A NEW REGIONAL POLICY FOR THE UK

John Adams, Peter Robinson
and Anthony Vigor

30-32 Southampton Street, London WC2E 7RA
Tel: 020 7470 6100 Fax: 020 7470 6111
info@ippr.org.uk
www.ippr.org
Registered charity 800065

The Institute for Public Policy Research (ippr), established in 1988, is Britain's leading independent think tank on the centre left. The values that drive our work include delivering social justice, deepening democracy, increasing environmental sustainability and enhancing human rights. Through our well-researched and clearly argued policy analysis, our publications, our media events, our strong networks in government, academia and the corporate and voluntary sector, we play a vital role in maintaining the momentum of progressive thought.

ippr's aim is to bridge the political divide between the social democratic and liberal traditions, the intellectual divide between the academics and the policy makers and the cultural divide between the policy-making establishment and the citizen. As an independent institute, we have the freedom to determine our research agenda. ippr has charitable status and is funded by a mixture of corporate, charitable, trade union and individual donations.

Research is ongoing, and new projects being developed, in a wide range of policy areas including sustainability, health and social care, social policy, citizenship and governance, education, economics, democracy and community, media and digital society and public private partnerships. We shall shortly open an office in Newcastle: ippr north.

For further information you can contact ippr's external affairs department on info@ippr.org, you can view our website at www.ippr.org and you can buy our books from Central Books on 0845 458 9910 or email ippr@centralbooks.com.

Production & design by **EMPHASIS**
ISBN 1 86030 224 6
© IPPR 2003

Contents

Foreword
Acknowledgements
About the authors

Executive summary   i

1.   Introduction   1

2.   The scale of the challenge   12

3.   Employment and regional policy   30

4.   The regional skills, education and training agenda   49

5.   Science, innovation and the regions   61

6.   Enterprise policy   71

7.   Public spending and investment   79

8.   Governance issues   93

9.   A modern regional economic policy   102

     References   105

Foreword

For those of us who have been immersed in regional policy debates for many years the recent renaissance has been heartening. One of the most persistent characteristics of the geography of the UK is the wide inequality that exists between its constituent nations and regions. It is an inequality that has come to be known as the 'north-south divide', and which is on many measures getting considerably worse.

The causes of regional economic disparities are numerous and wide-ranging. Some of its roots are clearly in deep-seated historical trends – including the shift in the direction of UK trade from westwards to south eastwards, from Atlantic to Europe and the decline in industries once central to the livelihoods of so many regions in the 'North' (textiles, coalmining, shipbuilding *et al*). However, the 'north-south divide' is not a result of 'market forces' alone – it has been exacerbated by social and political forces which could have been (and could still be) different.

This situation will not change unless there is a more serious engagement with the power dynamics that underlie the fundamentally unequal and undemocratic geography of the United Kingdom. In the absence of a systematic attack on the spatial concentration of power, the concessions on offer in the current debates will amount to little more than a pin-prick in tackling the alarming regional inequality that currently exists in the UK.

There is much one could criticise in New Labour's new regionalism, but at least we have a Government with an explicit commitment to reducing regional economic disparities. Whether HM Treasury appreciates the scale and nature of the challenge they have set themselves is another question entirely. What is required is a fundamental shift in the geography of the governing of the country. Nor will results be achieved overnight – even with the best will in the world it will take decades seriously to tackle regional economic disparities in the UK.

The authors of this report have addressed the subject with a commendable and ambitious breadth and depth, challenging some accepted wisdoms and offering detailed analyses and practical ways forward. Excellent reports like these should inform the actions of policy-makers in this area.

Professor Doreen Massey
Professor of Geography, Open University

Acknowledgements

The Institute for Public Policy Research (ippr) would like to thank our project partners and sponsors. Without their willingness to invest and contribute to our research this project could not have been undertaken. Our thanks go to ESRC Devolution Programme; Housing Corporation; London Development Agency; North East Assembly; Northern Ireland Government Departments; North West Development Agency; One NorthEast; Yorkshire Forward.

The findings of our research are, however, the responsibility of the authors alone and do not necessarily represent the views of our funding partners or any other individual or organisation involved with the project.

We would like to thank all those who have contributed to the ideas contained in this report, through seminars and informal discussions. In particular: Harvey Armstrong (University of Sheffield); John Bachtler (Strathclyde University); David Charles (University of Newcastle); Steve Fothergill (Sheffield Hallam University); Andrew Glyn (Oxford University); Mark Goodwin (University of Aberystwyth); Cllr Steve Houghton (Leader of Barnsley Council); Alan Hughes (Cambridge Centre for Business Research); Andrew Hughes-Hallett (University of Cardiff); Charlie Jeffery (University of Birmingham); Iain McLean (Oxford University); Kevin Morgan (University of Cardiff); Neil Mundy (One NorthEast); Tom Riordan (Yorkshire Forward); Fred Robinson (University of Durham); David Storey (Warwick Business School); Adam Tickell (University of Bristol) and Michael Ward (London Development Agency).

Many officials in Whitehall and devolved and regional institutions provided significant contributions to the seminars and helpful general discussions. We are grateful they were able to find time within their busy schedules to contribute their knowledge. We respect their wish to remain anonymous.

We would also like to thank the following individuals from within ippr: Richard Brooks, Jesse Caplan, Tony Grayling, James Hulme, Rachel O'Brien, Sue Regan, Beatrice Stern, Helena Scott, and Matthew Taylor.

About the authors

John Adams is a Senior Research Fellow at the Institute for Public Policy Research (ippr). He is responsible for research in the areas of devolution and regional policy and is co-ordinating the creation of ippr north – ippr's new office in Newcastle.

John helped draw up the Labour Party proposals for a Welsh Assembly in the run-up to the 1997 General Election, and was a Special Advisor at the Welsh Office in 1997-98. He was a co-editor of the joint ippr/ESRC publication *Devolution in Practice*. He is a member of the Advisory Board of the ESRC Devolution programme and the Board of the Campaign for the English Regions (CFER) and is a Visiting Fellow at CURDS at the University of Newcastle.

Peter Robinson has been Senior Economist at the ippr since 1997. He leads the ippr team dealing with economic and employment policy issues and is also closely involved in the Institute's work on education and training policy.

He was co-author of ippr's report *Opportunity for Whom?* on the funding and structure of post-16 education; and co-author of *Building Better Partnerships*, the final report resulting from ippr's Commission on Public Private Partnerships. He is a Research Associate at the Centre for Economic Performance at the London School of Economics.

Anthony Vigor is Research Assistant in devolution and regional policy at the ippr. He joined ippr earlier this year from the University of Manchester were he undertook a PhD in the politics of regional economic development within the UK and US.

Anthony is particularly interested in issues of devolution, economic development, urban regeneration and community development, and has published articles in *Local Economy* and the *Municipal Journal*. Anthony has also worked extensively on the opening of ippr's new office in Newcastle.

Executive summary

The 'North' is poorer than the 'South'. Although some dispute the existence of a 'north-south gap' in prosperity, it is clear that within the UK there is a 'winner's circle' in the Greater South East of the UK (consisting of London, the East of England and South East regions and parts of the South West). The rest of the country has lower levels of prosperity, and three regions lag significantly: Northern Ireland, Wales and the North East of England.

There is a growing consensus that these regional disparities need to be tackled and a variety of reasons have forced this issue up the political agenda:

● the gap in regional prosperity has been growing since the economic recovery began in 1992-93;

● the enlargement of the EU will mean that after 2006 the poorer UK regions will cease to receive the same degree of EU Structural Funds on which they currently rely so heavily;

● the sustained regional voice provided by the Deputy Prime Minister has been supplemented by the rise of HM Treasury as champions of Labour's 'New Regional Policy'.

In the Spending Review of 2002, the Chancellor announced a new Public Spending Agreement (PSA) target to 'over the long term reduce the persistent gap in growth rates between the regions'. This is a highly significant shift in Government policy and is to be welcomed. However, it only applies to England when it should apply to the whole of the UK. Furthermore, it is a target to reduce the gap in growth rates, not to close absolute disparities. The Government might meet this target at the same time as regional economic disparities continue to grow.

The scale of the challenge

The headline measure of output or Gross Value Added (GVA) per head is not the only useful indicator for analysing regional economic disparities.

1. GVA is a function of differences in productivity *and* employment. The relative importance of each will vary from region to region. In lagging regions the numbers claiming benefits relating to sickness and disability dwarf those claiming benefits relating to unemployment.

2. There are clearly differences in prosperity *within* as well as *between* regions. However, GVA is an unreliable measure at this smaller spatial scale. A more obvious measure of economic prosperity at this scale is levels of employment.

3.   GVA is a measure of *output*, not a measure of *income* available to households. Transfer payments through the tax and benefit system reduce but do not eliminate regional disparities.

4.   The use of GVA fails to highlight London's high levels of child poverty, but tax and benefit policies are more important than regional policy instruments in tackling this problem.

5.   Using only GVA does nothing to indicate an individual's 'happiness'. This depends on such factors as income, employment and health. Significant regional disparities exist in each of these areas. Claims that the 'North' is poorer but happier than the 'South' are profoundly mistaken.

6.   Using GVA fails to take account of the condition of the natural environment. The Greater South East needs to address the immediate problems of success such as congestion. In lagging regions, the need to boost growth rates cannot privilege economic over environmental concerns.

The market is not acting effectively to reduce regional economic disparities. High costs in the 'South' should generate incentives for firms and people to locate to disadvantaged regions but public policy is currently blunting incentives to relocate by offsetting the problems faced by successful congested regions.

It is as unhelpful to argue that the 'South should be left to stew' as it is to argue that London 'drives' the UK economy. The role of London in the UK economy needs to be carefully addressed: most employment in London is not directly associated with international markets and there is a relationship of *interdependence* with the rest of the UK. Worrying about whether London drives the UK economy or vice-versa is pointless. The housing and transport needs of the Greater South East should be addressed, but this should be paid for within the region.

Employment and regional policy

Levels of employment vary significantly within and between regions. In the Greater South East there is a broad swathe of areas with close to full employment. Many lagging regions have much lower employment rates. Major cities, including London, also have low employment rates.

The most important dispute in regional economic policy is to what extent differences in employment rates reflect 'demand-side' or 'supply-side' problems. That is, whether there are differences in employment opportunities or whether unemployed people are unable to get the jobs which do exist. The Government would emphasise the latter and would claim that areas of high unemployment lie within easy travelling distance of areas where vacancies are plentiful.

However, there are areas with low levels of employment not within easy travelling distance of anywhere with a tight labour market. For example, Hartlepool borders Middlesborough and Stockton, and Sunderland and Durham. Similar observations can be made of Northern Ireland, West Wales and the Valleys and industrial West Cumbria.

On the other hand, the Treasury argument does carry some force in large metropolitan areas like London or Glasgow. Concentrations of non-employment in Hackney are not due to a lack of jobs locally. This misunderstands the way that the housing and labour markets work in London. Individuals who face barriers to securing employment are concentrated in certain areas where housing is cheaper or socially provided. They need support to help them overcome these barriers.

Worklessness in Hackney is different to worklessness in Hartlepool. There is no Hackney labour market, but there is a distinct Hartlepool labour market. The residents of Hackney need a robust London labour market and supply-side measures to help them access jobs across the whole of the metropolitan labour market. The residents of Hartlepool require similar supply-side measures, but combined with policy instruments designed to create more jobs within easy travelling distance.

Full employment requires a strong national economy, a strong regional policy, supply-side measures and measures to reduce residential segregation and the links between segregation and disadvantage.

For those regions with a concentration of Travel-To-Work Areas (TTWAs) with low employment rates, demand for labour needs to be stimulated. Assisted Areas should be defined on TTWAs (not wards) – nearby areas of potential growth should not be cut off from support. More emphasis needs to be placed on allocating RSA grants to service sector companies, to redress the bias towards manufacturing. There should be fewer prestige inward investment projects and more support for the creation and expansion of smaller indigenous enterprises

Eastward expansion of the EU after 2006 is likely to cut the Structural Funds available to lagging regions. The UK Government has advocated a 'renationalisation' of regional policy and has guaranteed that domestic regional funding would be increased (although it is unclear to what extent). The European Commission should support this approach. The EU target of 70 per cent of the adult workforce in employment by 2010 should provide an important 'floor target' for domestic regional policy. UK Government resources could then be targeted on those TTWAs with employment rates at or below 70 per cent. This could consist of extra resources for RSA, but there should be the flexibility for regional and local agencies to choose what to fund.

The regional skills, education and training agenda

There is a fairly clear 'north-south gap' across the English regions in terms of qualifications: London and the South East have significantly higher proportions of the working age population with higher education qualifications and lower proportions of the population with no qualifications.

This gap is a consequence of differences in educational attainment at 16 and staying on rates post-16, but is also a consequence of out-migration of the better qualified to more prosperous regions, where a higher proportion of better jobs is on offer.

Recent moves to regionalise the local Learning and Skills Councils' budgets are a red herring: it is impossible for the public sector to plan to match the skills of the workforce to the demands of employers. Individuals should make their own decisions over further education and training. RDAs should focus on increasing the demand for skills from employers, in itself a very difficult agenda.

One recent issue flagged up by the Chancellor is whether the UK has sufficient regional and local variation in pay. Although national pay setting is the norm in both the private and the public sector, in practice there is much local discretion to reflect local circumstances.

In general the labour market does not seem to be failing in a profound way to allocate labour efficiently across the regions, although there are specific problems including parts of the public sector. Successful congested regions should bear the costs of higher pay for public sector workers.

Science, innovation and the regions

Innovation policy has been driven by vague concepts, such as the creation of a 'knowledge-based economy' and other fashionable ideas. An evidence-based approach should replace the 'guru-led' approach we have at present.

One of the reasons why this has not happened is the paucity of good evidence from rigorous evaluation. A large element of innovation policy should be focused on dissemination and on what must seem rather mundane initiatives, such as human resource management or modest improvements in management practice. At present we do not even have a methodology by which to measure such things.

The most common proxy for innovation is spending on Research and Development (R&D) and there are clear regional differences in business, higher education and directly government-funded R&D.

A different picture emerges from the UK Innovation Survey, which concluded that there were few substantial differences between regions. This survey is still in its infancy but its results should not be dismissed as too counter-intuitive. It may be that firms in the 'North' are not less innovative but that there are less of them.

There are very clear regional divides in science spending. A common question is whether the science base should be regionalised with spending more evenly spread across the UK? This is not an easy issue and difficult trade-offs need to be managed: funding science in the Greater South East might exacerbate regional economic differentials; regionalising the science base could harm the standing of UK science. There will not always be a 'win-win' situation. A centre-left government should prioritise regional policy and full-employment.

Some science institutions should be relocated from the Greater South East to lagging regions. This would help create jobs, and it may lead to a culture change that would address the concentration of science spending in the South East. Suggested institutions include the seven research councils and the Higher Education Funding Council for England. New investment in science could also be 'top-sliced' to create a regional science fund.

Enterprise policy

In the UK, debates about enterprise are too focused on small and medium sized enterprises (SMEs). In truth, enterprise policy is as relevant to large firms as to small firms. While SMEs create a large number of new jobs, it is also subject to large-scale job losses. Notably, a higher proportion of the workforce is employed in SMEs in lagging Northern Ireland and Wales than in 'prosperous' London. There seems little correlation between firm size and regional prosperity.

Nearly £8 billion is spent on public sector support for SMEs: £3 billion by DEFRA on agricultural support, £2.6 billion by the Treasury on revenue foregone through tax measures, and £2.2 billion on other initiatives. This £2.2 billion is spent on a complicated and inefficient array of initiatives, particularly external business advice. A pilot scheme is currently in operation where four RDAs are leading the co-ordination and management of Business Links. It may be too early to judge their success, but the case for RDAs assuming responsibility is strong.

A great deal of research has tried to establish the characteristics of the more successful entrepreneur. One conclusion is that age is an important determinant, and the easiest way to promote enterprise is to focus on individuals in their 30s or 40s who are well educated and who have experience of working in a particular sector.

Social enterprise has moved up the political and policy agenda in recent years, but it is not clear how useful it is in improving economic activity or creating jobs. Enterprise Areas are also a recent creation. Their boundaries are drawn at the ward level (postcode level in Scotland). However, these deprived areas are unlikely to have a high proportion of the professionals likely to make successful entrepreneurs. A focus on broader TTWAs would be more likely to ensure that Enterprise Areas cover potential entrepreneurs. Those in 'hard-to-reach' communities may start a business but, crucially, they would also be within travelling distance should other entrepreneurs create job opportunities.

Public spending and investment

Despite the significant variations in public expenditure across the nations and regions of the UK, there is little political likelihood of reforming the so-called Barnett formula. Nevertheless, this debate will not go away and there are many other public expenditure issues which are relevant to current debates.

The basic principle of fiscal equalisation must be that any particular area should be able to offer its residents broadly the same level of public services as another area regardless of its economic prosperity or the tax base. From each region according to their means, to each according to their 'needs'.

Defining 'needs' is an inherently difficult task but any fair formula would take into account:

- the total population

- well-recognised needs such as child poverty or ill-health

- other needs such as the problems posed by high levels of mobility and transience

- the higher costs of delivering public services in rural areas

- more controversially, the higher costs of delivering public services in congested regions

Some elements of higher spending will, however, reflect conscious policy choices and these costs should be borne locally, for example in relation to free personal care in Scotland.

It is important to recognise that central government can ensure fiscal equalisation without controlling a majority of public expenditure. It can balance 'needs' across different territories with only 25-30 per cent of total funding, allowing more revenue to be raised locally.

Policy is nudging in this direction, and there do seem to be moves to get some of the problems of congestion paid for locally. Congestion charging in London is the highest profile initiative, and it has been suggested that some of the costs of Crossrail could be funded regionally. Furthermore, it seems as if the Office of the Deputy Prime Minister (ODPM) wishes to try to capture more of the increased value of development in housing for the public purse. Such moves are welcome and should be further developed.

The Lyons Review of public sector relocation for HM Treasury has to be done in a manner compatible with the needs of the lagging regions. As they have a shortage of high-quality graduate jobs, back-room posts cannot be all that is relocated. If entire departments or agencies, for example the Office of the Deputy Prime Minister, the Department for Education and Skills and the Department of Health, are moved senior posts would have to be relocated. Lagging regions also need higher levels of R&D, so institutions which could be relocated in this field include the Higher Education Funding Council and the seven Research Councils. This would be an important job creation measure, but it would also help change the cultural attitudes that disproportionately fund science in the Greater South East.

Governance issues

One of the distinguishing features of the current renaissance in regional economic policy has been its emphasis on increased capacity at the regional level: bottom-up not top-down. This is clearly correct, as regional policy cannot be solely run from the centre. However, regional assemblies are a necessary but not sufficient reform for reducing economic disparities. The record of Whitehall in this field is far from distinguished.

A bottom-up regional economic policy does not mean that central government does not retain a responsibility for all parts of the UK: it cannot merely 'pass the buck'. The commitment by central government to a target of reducing regional economic disparities is a welcome recognition of this.

Policies must be designed and administered at the best spatial scale if we are to have the effective delivery of public policy. Otherwise, services will poorly delivered and taxpayers money wasted: square pegs do not fit round holes. 'Joined-up government' has received much attention in recent years. However, the spatial debate has received much less attention, and needs to precede debates on joined-up governance.

For example, it is wrong to try to create jobs in deprived localities as this misunderstands the way in which the labour market works. It is more effective to create jobs in areas attractive to employers but within travelling distance of deprived communities. Good quality transport links would ensure job opportunities are available to individuals in areas with high levels of economic inactivity.

Whitehall has a well-deserved reputation for being regionally insensitive. Its role of balancing the different and often competing interests of the different parts of the UK is difficult. On balance, it seems as if Whitehall does not sufficiently prioritise the needs of lagging regions although we do recognise the needs of London particularly in the area of child poverty. Whitehall must 'mainstream' the regional agenda into their spending decisions so that policies in areas such as housing, transport and science policy reduce regional disparities, not reinforce them. The 2004 Spending Review will be the key test as to whether it is moving in the right direction.

A modern regional economic policy

The ten-point plan for regional economic policy outlined below is deliberately not a set of new spending commitments as we recognise that in the context of the 2004 Spending Review resources are constrained. Instead, it flags up some difficult issues that need to be addressed and priorities that need to be established.

Ten point plan for regional economic policy

1 The 2004 Spending Review should set out an unambiguous target to narrow disparities in output per head across the UK nations and regions. The Joint Ministerial Committee on the Economy taking place later in 2003 should be used to agree a target between the Government and devolved administrations.

2 Employment should be given equal weight with productivity as the focus for regional economic policy. Policies are required to increase the demand for labour in the Assisted Areas, which should be re-defined to cover groups of Travel-To-Work Areas in lagging regions with employment rates at or below 70 per cent so that regional policy instruments can be concentrated.

3 The EU should back the UK position of 'renationalising' regional policy. HM Treasury needs to commit significant additional resources to compensate lagging regions for lower levels of EU spending. Regional and local institutions must decide how that funding is allocated across different areas of spending.

4 More good quality jobs need to be created in lagging regions to retain graduates. Increasing the proportion of young people and adults with adequate basic skills and level 2 qualifications are the correct priorities for promoting employment. A period of stability in the administration of learning and skills policy is required.

5 The Government should 'regionalise the science base' by relocating key institutions and by 'top-slicing' new spending on science for lagging regions. The current concentration of government R&D spending and science institutions in the Greater South East is inequitable.

6 The Government needs to rationalise services for small and medium sized enterprises as the number of initiatives and bodies in this area are impossibly complex. In particular, if the current pilots are successful the case for RDAs assuming responsibility for Business Links will be very strong.

7 All Whitehall departments need to 'mainstream' the regional dimension into their spending decisions. Decisions in areas such as housing, transport and science policy need to reduce regional disparities not reinforce them.

---

8 Prosperous regions and localities should bear more of the costs of extra spending required to deal with the problems of success. Congestion charging and capturing increases in land values can only be the start of something bigger in terms of fiscal reform.

9 Several Departments and Agencies should be relocated from the Greater South East to the lagging regions, such as the ODPM, the Higher Education Funding Council for England and the seven Research Councils. The Lyons Review must relocate senior staff as well as back-room staff.

10 A central research unit for the RDAs and the Core Cities should be created to help promote evidence-based policy-making. This should be located in one of the lagging regions.

1. Introduction

The 'North' is poorer than the 'South'. Though some have sought to question the existence of any 'north-south divide', as Figure 1.1 clearly demonstrates, there are clear and significant regional economic differentials within the UK.[1] Levels of output, as measured using Gross Value Added (GVA), are well above the national average in a 'winner's circle' in the Greater South East (consisting of London, the East of England and South East regions and parts of the South West). The rest of the country has lower levels of prosperity, and three regions lag significantly: Northern Ireland, Wales and the North East of England.

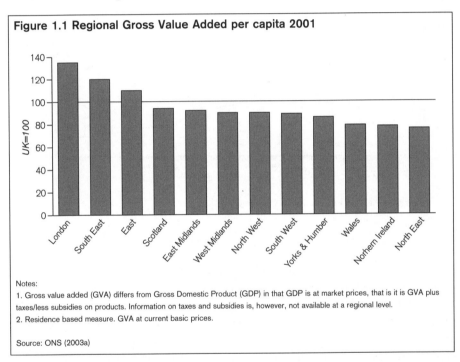

Figure 1.1 Regional Gross Value Added per capita 2001

Notes:
1. Gross value added (GVA) differs from Gross Domestic Product (GDP) in that GDP is at market prices, that is it is GVA plus taxes/less subsidies on products. Information on taxes and subsidies is, however, not available at a regional level.
2. Residence based measure. GVA at current basic prices.

Source: ONS (2003a)

There is a growing consensus that these regional disparities need to be tackled and a variety of reasons have forced this issue up the political agenda. Improving the performance of the poorer regions is the key to achieving full employment nationally and to improving the UK's relative productivity. Not only is it a waste of talent and opportunity for the economies of some regions and countries to fall behind, this situation can exacerbate the already substantial pressures on housing and land-use in the Greater South East. Unbalanced growth can undermine national economic performance and a strong regional economic policy is therefore important for promoting *economic efficiency*.

1   In this report we shall sometimes refer to the nations of Scotland, Wales and Northern Ireland as 'regions'. This is not to diminish their important cultural and political distinction from the regions of England but unfortunately it is a necessary aid to comprehension.

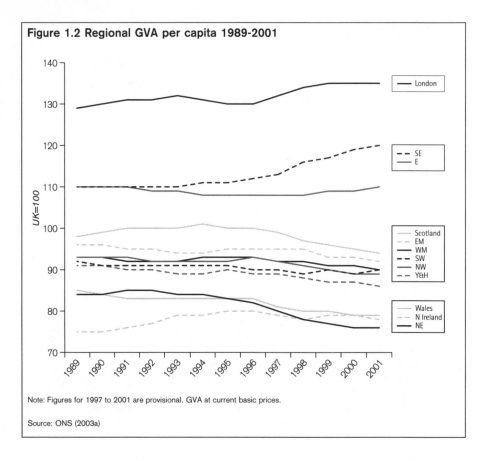

Figure 1.2 Regional GVA per capita 1989-2001

Note: Figures for 1997 to 2001 are provisional. GVA at current basic prices.

Source: ONS (2003a)

However, there is also a straightforward *equity* case for a strong regional economic policy: reducing disparities in prosperity across the UK is important for improving the quality of life of individuals. It is unacceptable, particularly for the centre-left, that life chances should be different depending on which region of the country a person is born in. Those in the lagging regions suffer from a shorter life and fewer economic opportunities, while those in the Greater South East suffer from a lower quality of life than necessary due to overcrowding and congestion.

While not all inequalities are unjust, those that are need to be tackled and eliminated. The systemic regional economic disparities that have existed in the UK for generations are quite clearly inequitable. The perception that national UK-wide institutions have systematically failed to address this problem exacerbates the sense of injustice. This also undermines our *solidarity* as a nation, as sharp disparities undermine the sense of citizenship and cohesion that create a national polity.

In the last few years there has been a remarkable renewal of interest in regional economic policy (for example, Balls and Healey 2000, Regional Studies Association

2001, Amin *et al* 2003). A number of factors have contributed to the rise of regional issues:

- Despite reasonable overall economic growth in the UK, the gap between the 'North' and 'South' has been growing since the beginning of the economic recovery in 1992-3 (see Figure 1.2).

- The devolution of power to Scotland, Wales, Northern Ireland and London has institutionalised the territorial dimension in UK politics. The possible move towards elected assemblies in the three northern regions of England will give added impetus to territorial politics within the UK.

- The enlargement of the EU will mean that after 2006 the poorer UK regions will cease to receive the same degree of EU Structural Funds on which they currently rely so heavily. UK regional policy will therefore have to be, at least to some extent, 're-nationalised'.

- Perhaps most importantly, within the Cabinet, the sustained regional voice provided by the Deputy Prime Minister has been supplemented by the rise of HM Treasury as champions of Labour's 'New Regional Policy', developed during its first term in office (see, for example, Balls and Healey 2000).

In the Spending Review of 2002, the Chancellor announced a new Public Spending Agreement (PSA) target to:

> make sustainable improvements in the economic performance of all English regions and over the long term reduce the persistent gap in growth rates between the regions, defining measures to improve performance and reporting progress against these measures by 2006 (HMT 2002a)

This target with its commitment to reduce the gap between the *English* regions represented a significant shift in Government policy, which as set out in a 2000 PSA target was to 'improve the economic performance of *all* regions' (emphasis added, see Table 1.1). This approach had been criticised for not truly being a regional economic policy, in the sense of targeting the lagging regions in order to narrow gaps in economic prosperity. It was more akin to a national economic development strategy, albeit partly regionally administered, that treated unequal regions equally.

The 2002 PSA target is in principle a radical commitment with enormous implications. The HM Treasury/DTI report *Productivity in the UK: 3 – The Regional Dimension* (*Productivity 3*) concluded that 'Whilst regional economic policy must aim to strengthen the indigenous growth potential of all regions, the focus should be on the weakest regions, without constraining the strongest' (HMT/DTI 2001). This is clearly the correct approach. It is sometimes argued that development controls in the 'South' could be tightened to induce capital to move north (Morgan 2002). At the heart of this 'donor-recipient' model is the influential Barlow Report (1940) which argued that over- and under- development are two sides of the same coin. However, restricting the supply of land in the 'South', for whatever reason, cannot guarantee that capital will indeed travel north but can guarantee that land and house prices in the 'South' will increase.

It will be the poor who would suffer from such a policy: in the 'South' it would be the least advantaged who would have the greatest difficulty in paying increased housing costs, and for those in the 'North' the option of inter-regional migration will be even less likely. The wealthy (from both 'North' and 'South') would be better able to cope with the implications of development controls. There may be very valid environmental reasons to restrict some development in the 'South' to maintain and enhance quality of life, but we have to question the implications for economic development. Therefore (with the exception of public sector institutions discussed in Chapter 7) the emphasis should not be on 'push' factors but on 'pull' factors.

In the words of the Nine English Regional Development Agencies (2003) in their response to the ODPM Select Committee inquiry into reducing regional disparities, 'There will, however, inevitably be the need to exercise some forms of *positive discrimination* in certain policy areas to help raise the performance of the lagging regions' (emphasis added). The form of desirable positive discrimination that might be required in certain policy areas is discussed throughout this report.

A framework for analysis

Before examining the detail of policy, it is necessary to set out a clear conceptual framework for thinking about and accounting for regional disparities in prosperity. Much of the Government's focus on regional economic disparities seems to stem from its concern with the UK's productivity gap in relation to some comparable countries. This is why it is important to view the regional PSA target in the light of the target to narrow the productivity gap (see Table 1.1). We think this is a fundamentally limiting approach in terms of both the analysis of the regional problem and the range of policies necessary to address that problem. Most importantly, it downgrades the importance of disparities in employment across the UK's regions, though increasing employment rates is also a key Government target.

It is also clear that the framework used by the Government to think about differences in productivity across *countries* has severe limitations as a way of thinking about differences in prosperity across *regions*. When addressing national economic performance, the Government makes much use of the five drivers of productivity it has identified: skills, enterprise, innovation, competition and investment. However,

Table 1.1 PSA targets and regional policy		
1998 Spending Review	*2000 Spending Review*	*2002 Spending Review*
	'improve the economic performance of all regions measured by the trend in growth of each region's GDP per capita' *DETR, DTI*	'make sustainable improvements in the economic performance of all English regions and over the long term reduce the persistent gap in growth rates between the regions, defining measures to improve performance and reporting progress against these measures by 2006' *ODPM, DTI, HMT*
'to put in place policies to narrow the productivity gap relative to other industrialised countries over the cycle' *DTI, HMT*	'improve UK competitiveness by narrowing the productivity gap with the US, France, Germany and Japan over the economic cycle' *DTI, HMT*	'demonstrate progress by 2006 on the Government's long-term objective of raising the rate of UK productivity growth over the economic cycle, improving competitiveness and narrowing the productivity gap with the US, France and Germany' *DTI, HMT*
'helping people into work; in particular by helping young people, the long-term unemployed and others at a disadvantage in the labour market, including lone parents, to move into sustainable jobs, within a fair and diverse employment market.' *DfES*	'over the 3 years to 2004 increase the employment rates of disadvantaged areas and groups, taking account of the economic cycle – people with disabilities, lone parents, ethnic minorities and the over 50s, the 30 local authority districts with the poorest initial labour market position - and reduce the difference between their employment rates and the overall rate' *DfES*	'over the three years to Spring 2006, increase the employment rates of disadvantaged areas and groups, taking account of the economic cycle – lone parents, ethnic minorities, people aged 50 and over, those with the lowest qualifications, and the 30 local authority districts with the poorest initial labour market position, and significantly reduce the difference between their employment rates and the overall employment rate.' *DWP*

Government documents (including the *Productivity 3* report) seem to struggle to make this framework fit easily with an analysis of regional disparities. Furthermore, these five productivity drivers miss out some of the most important drivers of prosperity at a regional and local level, specifically, the efficiency with which labour and housing markets operate. We should aim to have a conceptual framework that allows these two critical issues to be addressed.

Our framework is set out in Figure 1.3. In the most straightforward framework,

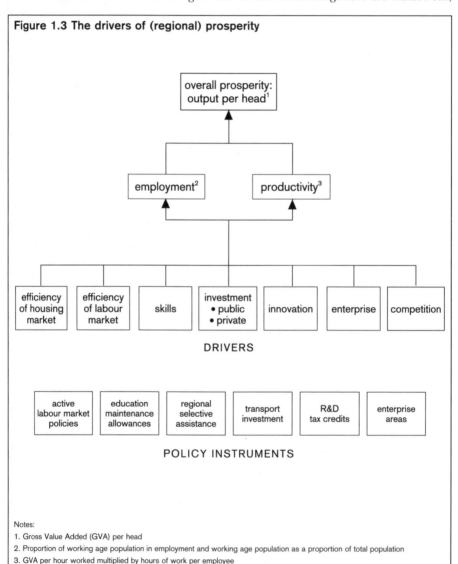

Figure 1.3 The drivers of (regional) prosperity

overall prosperity: output per head[1]

employment[2]

productivity[3]

| efficiency of housing market | efficiency of labour market | skills | investment • public • private | innovation | enterprise | competition |

DRIVERS

| active labour market policies | education maintenance allowances | regional selective assistance | transport investment | R&D tax credits | enterprise areas |

POLICY INSTRUMENTS

Notes:
1. Gross Value Added (GVA) per head
2. Proportion of working age population in employment and working age population as a proportion of total population
3. GVA per hour worked multiplied by hours of work per employee

differences in overall prosperity as measured by output per head are accounted for by differences in productivity and in employment. In turn, it is useful to think about the drivers of those two important outcomes, which would include the Government's five productivity drivers and also the efficient operation of labour and housing markets. It is important to stress that a driver like skills may be important for both productivity and employment. We can also think of a wide range of policy instruments, of which only a few are shown in Figure 1.3, that might impact on the drivers of employment and productivity. We think this represents a much fuller picture for thinking about the causes of and potential solutions to regional economic disparities.

The principles of regional policy

There are five key objectives that must be at the heart of future regional policy for the UK as a whole.

1. **Making territorial justice an integral part of delivering social and economic justice for individuals**

   The territorial dimension is of vital importance to effective public policy. Although the welfare of individuals is at the core of the concept of social justice, the argument that 'it's people who are poor, not places' misses the impact that geographical situation can have on life chances. If we are to develop a clear understanding of the different regional economies within the UK and how the gaps in prosperity might be narrowed then we must start with an understanding of the role of territory in public policy.

2. **Reducing the long-term differentials in regional economic performance**

   As we have argued above, reducing regional economic differentials is important for promoting economic efficiency, for producing a more equitable distribution of prosperity and for underpinning our solidarity as a nation.

3. **Designing industrial and urban policies to meet different regional needs**

   It is right that governments should have the twin objectives of both increasing the economic performance of the nation as a whole and striving to ensure equity in regional economic performance. This implies both effective national economic and regional economic policies. However, it is equally important that governments understand the interaction between these different policies, that there may be times when they conflict, and come to terms with the difficult trade-offs that this entails. Furthermore, national and regional economic policies also interact with other policy tools. For example, regeneration initiatives such as the Neighbourhood Renewal Fund and the New Deal for Communities are in large part focused on poorer regions, and so could contribute towards reducing regional economic disparities.

4.   **Developing a more sophisticated understanding of regional disparities, and not simply relying on GDP/GVA per head**

GDP or GVA per head is the best measure of regional economic performance that exists. It is, however, only a relatively narrow measure of economic performance. In addition to maintaining economic growth and improving living standards, we must address the social and environmental problems facing our society. Ultimately, the state of our society should be judged, not in terms of economic goals alone but in terms of quality of life. Regional policy in the future must have a more subtle understanding of issues such as environmental sustainability, individual welfare or 'happiness'.

5.   **Developing the quasi-federal role of the UK government to balance the needs of the UK's nations and regions**

The Government must develop its quasi-federal role if it is to effectively address inter-regional disparities (Adams and Robinson 2002). Such a role is entirely compatible with the principle of devolution and the Government's 'bottom-up' approach to regional development. But there will be relative winners and losers if regional policy is to adequately address inter-regional disparities.

Current regional economic priorities

We have acknowledged that the Government has made considerable progress in developing its regional economic policy. In particular the setting of a Public Service Agreement target for narrowing the persistent gap in growth rates has been a major step forward. There has been much criticism of the Whitehall culture of target-setting, with observers rightly pointing out that targets can create some perverse incentives for public service organisations to concentrate on what is being measured and with the potential for some unintended adverse side effects. However, PSA targets are an important indicator of the Government's policy priorities and have a major impact in terms of concentrating minds in Whitehall. The 2002 PSA target of narrowing regional disparities has led to questions being asked about the regional impact of policies across a range of Whitehall departments. This in itself is a positive outcome.

It has also led to questions being asked about the statistical and evidence base for regional economic policy. The Office for National Statistics had to suspend their regional output statistics before publishing a new series in August 2003. A major enquiry into the quality of ONS regional statistics being conducted by Christopher

Allsopp, a former member of the Monetary Policy Committee, was due to be published in Autumn 2003. One issue on which there is wide consensus is the need for a significant improvement in the quality of regional data.

Unfortunately Whitehall has a habit of setting PSA targets and only then figuring out how to measure progress towards them. The current target on narrowing regional disparities has also been criticised for lacking ambition. To see why we have to look carefully at its wording.

The 2002 PSA target has three key components:

1.   Make sustainable improvements in the economic performance of *all English* regions (emphasis added)

2.   Over the long term reduce the persistent gap in *growth rates* between the regions (emphasis added)

3.   Define measures to improve performance and report progress against these measures by 2008.

The first component of the 2002 target is a rewording of the heavily criticised 2000 PSA target. This was criticised because it seemed to encourage *all* the English regions to improve their trend growth rates and so was not about narrowing regional disparities at all. The South East region could increase its growth rate by 0.5 per cent and the North East by 0.25 per cent and the target could be met, but of course regional economic disparities would continue to get worse.

Additionally, the first component only refers to the English regions. Of the three departments that own the PSA target, HM Treasury is a UK department and the DTI is a 'hybrid' department, exercising significant reserved powers on behalf of the UK. However, the target to narrow the gaps in regional prosperity excludes Scotland, Wales and Northern Ireland. If a commitment to equity between the regions of the UK is at the heart of the Government's approach – and as a centre-left government, it should be – then the exclusion of some national territories is puzzling.

The second component of the 2002 target *appears* to answer the criticism of the 2000 target, as it focuses on reducing the gap in *growth rates* between the regions. However, it should be emphasised that the target is not a commitment to reduce *absolute* disparities in prosperity between the regions, though HM Treasury and the DTI have elsewhere committed themselves to reducing *absolute* disparities in regional prosperity. The *Productivity 3* report identifies 'the Government's long-term ambition of reducing the persistent gap between regions by increasing the growth rate of the worst performing regions' (HMT/DTI 2001: 55). This ambition does not, however, have the impact of a PSA target.

To see why the 2002 PSA target does not commit the Government to reducing absolute disparities we must look at the estimates of trend growth rates in GVA per head in the regions contained in Table 1.2. The first column shows DTI estimates made in the first half of 2003 of trend growth rates for the English regions. Two points can be made. First, it is worrying that as a UK department the DTI feels under no obligation to provide statistical evidence on a consistent basis for all the UK's nations and regions: federal departments in all federal countries are obliged to produce data consistently for all parts of that country.

Second, if these estimates are correct, if the South East increased its growth rate by 0.25 per cent and the North East by 0.5 per cent, this would narrow regional disparities in growth rates as the second component of the 2002 PSA target demands. However, GVA per head in the South East would still be growing at 2.75 per cent per annum compared with 1.75 per cent in the North East, so absolute disparities in GVA per head would still be widening. The Government would claim to be meeting its PSA target and its critics would point out that the 'north-south gap' was still growing. In fact this seems a rather likely outcome.

Table 1.2 Estimated trend growth rate in GVA per head in the English regions and the UK's nations

UK nations and regions	% per annum over the 1990s	
	DTI	EBS
South East	2.5	2.5
East	2.25	2.25
London	2.0	1.5
Average	2.25	2.05
West Midlands	2.0	2.0
East Midlands	2.0	2.0
Yorkshire and Humber	2.0	2.0
South West	1.75	2.0
North West	1.50	1.75
North East	1.25	1.75
Average	1.75	1.95
Scotland	Not available	2.0
Northern Ireland	Not available	2.0
Wales	Not available	1.5
UK/England average	2.0	2.0

Note: These estimates were made before the August 2003 revisions to GVA data.

Source: DTI; Experian Business Strategies (2003)

However, there is a further point to be made about the 2002 PSA target. Estimating trend growth rates is an art even at the national level; at the regional level where the data is so poor this is even more the case. There is in fact little agreement over what the trend rates of growth of GVA per head are in the English regions. The second column of Table 1.2 has different estimates of growth rates for the English regions and also for the other nations of the UK. There is a particularly big gap between the two different estimates for London and for the North East, that is for the UK's richest and poorest regions. Also if we average out the estimates for the trend growth rates in the three regions making up the Greater South East and for the rates in the six lagging regions, the DTI estimates suggest there is some ground to make up between the two sets of regions. However, if we average out the estimates in the second column, there is in fact little difference in the trend growth rates between the two sets of regions.

So the Government has given itself a target to meet where:

a.   there is little agreement about how to measure whether the target is being met, and

b.   even if the target is met, in theory and probably in practice absolute disparities in prosperity between the 'North' and 'South' could get worse.

Conclusion: a new PSA target for 2004?

This leads to the obvious conclusion that the Government needs to develop a new PSA target for the 2004 Spending Review. Although the Office for National Statistics has had a troubling period with regard to its numbers on *levels* of GVA per head across the regions, this measure is likely to be much less difficult to get agreement on than a measure of the trend rate of *growth*. The level of GVA per head across the regions – a measure of the absolute 'north-south divide' – is also the measure that is salient politically, along with, as we argue in Chapter 2, differences in employment.

The Government has made considerable progress in developing its regional economic policy, but it needs to go further. The 2004 Spending Review should set out an unambiguous target to narrow disparities in GVA per head across the UK's regions. This should involve discussions between HMT and the DTI and the DWP, and the Scottish Executive and Welsh Assembly Government (and the political process permitting, the Northern Ireland Executive) and the ODPM and English regional bodies. The Joint Ministerial Committee on the Economy proposed to take place later in 2003 would provide an obvious venue for these discussions and a test case of how the UK's new system of governance can link the reserved and devolved economic policy agendas. What such a target would mean and what policy levers would be needed to deliver this, or indeed the current, PSA target, is the focus of the rest of this report.

2. The scale of the challenge

In Chapter 1 we argued that the UK Government and the devolved administrations should adopt a target that would address closing *absolute* disparities in prosperity across the UK's regions. This would be measured using the indicator of GVA per head at the level of the 12 nations and regions of the UK, a measure that is very close to the familiar indicator of GDP per head. Even if this, at first sight rather traditional, approach was to be accepted, a number of questions still need to be answered.

- Why does this report choose GDP or GVA per head as the key measure of progress, if one of the five key objectives of a strong regional economic policy is 'developing a more sophisticated understanding of regional disparities, and not simply relying on GDP/GVA per head'. In this chapter we wish to start exploring what this means, and will consider regional economic disparities from other perspectives.

- Why choose the *region* as the unit of analysis given that there is considerable variation in economic prosperity *within* regions? A variant of this concern is whether we should give more attention to the role of cities within our regions.

- How far is GDP or GVA per head a good measure of actual *living standards* in the regions, especially given the widely observed differences in the *cost of living* across the regions?

- Should we focus more on measures such as levels of relative *poverty* in the regions, especially important given the Government's flagship objective of abolishing child poverty by 2020?

- What can we learn from using other measures of wellbeing, including the growing literature on *'happiness'*, in particular with regard to health and especially mental health?

- How can the regional policy debate take more seriously the range of issues relating to *environmental* sustainability?

GVA per head, employment and productivity

Table 2.1 uses the most up-to-date figures that were available from official sources in the summer of 2003 to examine how differences in GVA per head across the UK's regions in 2001 were a function of differences in productivity *and* employment. The data reveals the well known 'north-south divide' at the regional level. It also demonstrates that the relative importance of employment and productivity in explaining disparities in GVA per head differs from region to region. The *Productivity*

3 report argued that, on average, productivity differentials accounted for around 60 per cent of regional differences in GVA per head, with the implication that the remaining 40 per cent reflected differences in employment. However, it also acknowledged that a striking feature of the UK regions with the lowest GVA per head – Wales, the North East and Northern Ireland – was a particularly poor labour market performance, with very low employment rates. On the other hand, the South West has above average levels of employment, but relatively poor productivity (and a low working age population share). London's relative prosperity is due to its very high levels of productivity and its high working age population share, despite mediocre rates of employment for those of working age.

Table 2.1 Three indices for regional prosperity (UK=100)

UK nations and regions	Employment rate as proportion of working age population 2001	Productivity levels GDP per person employed, 2001	Output levels GVA per person of working age, 2001, residence based
London	95	134	127
South East	108	111	120
East	106	103	111
Scotland	98	95	93
East Midlands	102	90	92
South West	107	86	92
West Midlands	100	92	91
North West	96	94	91
Yorkshire & Humberside	99	88	87
Wales	93	87	81
Northern Ireland	91	88	79
North East	92	84	77
United Kingdom	100	100	100

Source: Labour Force Survey 2001, ONS

There do seem to be wider disparities between the regions in terms of productivity than in employment, but it is not worth having a heated dispute about which accounts for more of the gaps in regional prosperity. Both are important in terms of analysing the problem. However, politically it seems clear that *employment* is viewed as the more pressing problem by those that live in the disadvantaged regions, for whom closing the productivity gap with the French is not obviously a salient issue.

The similar levels of employment in London and some of the northern English regions are somewhat deceptive: the problem of an area of low employment in an otherwise prosperous region is different in character to the problem of low employment in a disadvantaged region. As Chapter 3 will explore in detail, unemployed people in Hartlepool face very different hurdles to unemployed people in

Hackney. As the UK's richest region London best exemplifies the problem of a healthy overall jobs market co-existing with pockets of high unemployment. The barriers to employment here might include a lack of skills, a lack of information, poor transport or discrimination. Many government policy instruments are designed to tackle such supply-side problems: the New Deals and other active labour market policies; skills, education and training measures; and measures to tackle discrimination and promote equality. On the other hand, in Hartlepool such supply-side policies will not be fully effective in the absence of measures to raise the demand for labour, in the context of the simple observation that there are fewer job opportunities within reasonable travel-to-work distance.

This is not the only way in which the employment problem differs between the regions. Table 2.2 shows that the make up of the unemployed and inactive varies significantly across the UK's regions. In February 2003, nearly 15 per cent of adults of working age in Northern Ireland, nearly 14 per cent in Wales, nearly 13 per cent in the North East and 12 per cent in the North West were claiming benefits related to sickness and disability. These numbers dwarf those claiming benefits related to being unemployed and the contrast with the numbers in the East and South East regions is stark. Higher levels of claims related to sickness and disability account for nearly *three-quarters* of the gap between Northern Ireland and the South East in the overall proportion of working age adults claiming benefits. By contrast, London had the highest proportion of lone parent benefit claimants.

Another key feature of London's employment problem relates to the differences in employment by ethnic group. The employment rates for white adults and for all minority ethnic groups in London are strikingly similar to the employment rates for these groups for the UK as a whole. The employment rates for particular ethnic groups, including Indian, Pakistani and Bangladeshi, Black African and Black Caribbean are also very similar in the capital to the national average. Given that nearly half of all ethnic minority people live in London, this is not really surprising. However, it does lead to the observation that, in a strict accounting sense, London's relatively low employment rate is explained by having a much higher proportion of the working age population from minority ethnic backgrounds. This begs another set of questions about the range of barriers faced by minority ethnic groups in terms of their labour market participation in London and nationally (ippr 2003).

There are of course some obvious policy implications that result from these observations about how the nature of employment problems varies across the regions. The various New Deals – aimed at disabled people or lone parents for example – will be of differing importance in different regions, even if they are not explicitly targeted regionally. The differential effectiveness of the New Deals could have important regional implications. Active labour market policies are one type of policy instrument that need a regional perspective.

Table 2.2 Claimants of key benefits by statistical group and region, February 2003, as a percentage of the working age population

UK nations and regions	Statistical Group				
	all	unemployed	sick/ disabled	lone parents	others
North East	20.3	3.8	12.9	2.9	0.8
Wales	19.5	2.8	13.6	2.5	0.6
North West	18.1	2.9	11.9	2.7	0.6
Scotland	17.8	3.4	11.4	2.3	0.7
Yorkshire & Humberside	15.0	3.0	9.1	2.3	0.6
West Midlands	14.9	3.0	8.8	2.4	0.6
London	14.6	3.5	7.1	3.4	0.6
East Midlands	12.9	2.4	8.1	1.9	0.5
South West	10.9	1.8	7.0	1.7	0.4
East	10.0	1.8	5.9	1.9	0.4
South East	8.8	1.6	5.2	1.7	0.3
Great Britain	**14.2**	**2.7**	**8.7**	**2.3**	**0.5**
Northern Ireland	21.8	3.3	14.6	2.8	1.2

Note: Northern Ireland data had not been formally published at the time of writing, and was obtained directly from Northern Ireland Government Departments by the authors.

Source: DWP (2003: Table 6.2)

Why regions and not sub-regions or cities?

It is clear that there are significant differences in prosperity within as well as between regions. It is also clear that any 'north-south gap' in prosperity is overlaid and partly explained by an 'urban-rural' split, which is explored in more detail in Chapter 3 in relation to employment.

If, however, the focus for any policy is to narrow disparities in GDP or GVA per head, this should lead one to focus on the *region* as the correct unit of analysis, for the simple reason that GVA per head as a measure makes little sense below this level. This is partly because the EU defines sub-regions (NUTS level 2 in EU terminology) in such a manner that:

a.   leaves cities cut off from their hinterlands where much of their working population lives. This problem tends to exaggerate the GDP or GVA per head of many cities including, for example, Paris, Hamburg and Brussels (Boldrin and Canova 2001).

b.   cuts strange boundaries *within* cities such as London where Inner London is so defined as to include the financial and business services districts.

This problem is recognised by the UK Government. In *Productivity in the UK: 4 – the local dimension (Productivity 4)* (HMT/ODPM 2003) it was acknowledged, with regard to GDP per head, 'that comparisons of economic performance between areas become less precise as the areas under examination become geographically smaller'. This paper went on to say that 'it may be preferable to concentrate on other indicators when looking at living standards at a local level – for example, comparisons of household income'. We make this comparison at the regional level below.

For the cities of the UK, the more obvious measure of economic prosperity to concentrate on is employment, precisely because the main problem facing the cities is relatively low employment rates. Of the large English cities only Bristol (or strictly speaking the Travel-To-Work Area encompassing Bristol) could be described as a city at full employment, with an employment rate of over 80 per cent in 2001 (see Table 2.3). Of the remaining seven English 'core cities' only Leeds had an above average employment rate in 2001, along with Edinburgh. For employment it is indeed legitimate to look at one level of analysis below the region – the Travel-To-Work Area – and this forms the basis for much of the discussion in Chapter 3.

Table 2.3 Employment rates in the Core Cities, and other UK major cities, 2001	
	% of working age (16-59/64) population in employment
Bristol	80.9
Leeds	77.9
Nottingham	73.2
Sheffield	72.4
Manchester	72.4
Birmingham	70.8
Newcastle (Tyneside)	69.3
Liverpool	64.0
London	71.4
Cardiff	70.6
Glasgow	67.6
Belfast	67.2
Edinburgh	78.3

Note: Travel-To-Work Areas

Source: Labour Force Survey Local Area Database

The differences in employment rates between cities in Table 2.3 illustrate evidence for both a 'north-south gap' – with the low employment rates of Liverpool, Newcastle and Glasgow and Belfast standing out – but also emphasises the relative success of some northern cities (notably Leeds and Edinburgh) and the unique status of London. This clearly raises an important set of issues.

If it is correct that sub-regions (NUTS level 2) are not the right unit of analysis for looking at differences in GDP or GVA per head, this also allows us to clear up the strange point made in the *Productivity 3* report and elsewhere that regional disparities are worse in the UK than in other EU countries. Before looking at the evidence on this it is worth employing some intuition. A piece of analysis that tells us that the UK's regional disparities are worse than those in Italy makes little real sense. However, this is the conclusion that the analysis presented in *Productivity 3* leads us to, although it did acknowledge that 'Additional work needs to be done in this area'.

One way around the problems posed by the administrative boundaries that are used to define regions and sub-regions in the EU is presented below in Figure 2.1. This compares GDP per head for the most affluent regions where about 25 per cent of the population lives and the poorest regions where a further 25 per cent or so of the population lives, in the UK, Italy, France and Germany. It leads to the much more intuitively appealing result that Italy has the most severe regional disparities in prosperity, but that the UK, France and Germany face similar regional problems.

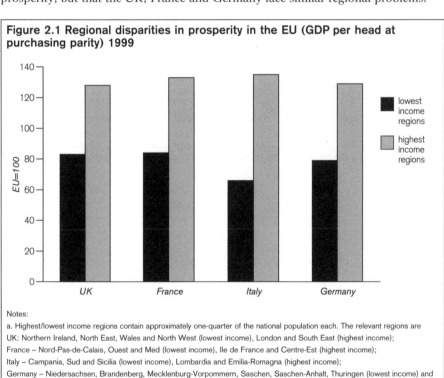

Figure 2.1 Regional disparities in prosperity in the EU (GDP per head at purchasing parity) 1999

Notes:

a. Highest/lowest income regions contain approximately one-quarter of the national population each. The relevant regions are UK: Northern Ireland, North East, Wales and North West (lowest income), London and South East (highest income); France – Nord-Pas-de-Calais, Ouest and Med (lowest income), Ile de France and Centre-Est (highest income); Italy – Campania, Sud and Sicilia (lowest income), Lombardia and Emilia-Romagna (highest income); Germany – Niedersachsen, Brandenberg, Mecklenburg-Vorpommern, Saschen, Saschen-Anhalt, Thuringen (lowest income) and Hamburg, Bremen, Bayern and Hessen (highest income).

b. Workplace based estimates are used, where the income of commuters is allocated to where they work.

c. UK estimates are provisional.

Source: Eurostat (2002); ONS (2002: Table 2.3) and authors' calculations

Part of the problem here seems to be that comparative analysis has trapped some policy makers into thinking that only if you can show the UK is worse off compared with other countries in some area of policy will this help justify taking action. We should want to address regional disparities in prosperity in the UK because of the social costs those disparities imply, not because of an – incorrect – assertion that the problem is so much worse in the UK than anywhere else.

Living standards and the cost of living

In the final analysis we are of course interested in the individual welfare of people as the ultimate policy goal. GVA is in principle a measure of the output being produced in each region. It is not, however, a measure of the income available to households in those regions. A significant source of household income in all the UK's regions consists of transfer payments through the tax and benefits system. A smoothly functioning modern welfare state will act to redistribute income from more prosperous individuals and regions towards poorer individuals and regions, thereby smoothing out economic disparities. GVA does not measure these payments, which are, of course, disproportionately important in the disadvantaged regions.

One measure which does take into account transfer payments is 'gross disposable household income per head', and the regional breakdown (for the late 1990s) is detailed in Table 2.4. This shows that the transfer payments managed by central government do have the effect of significantly reducing regional disparities. The gap of

---

Table 2.4 Gross disposable household income per head, three-year average, 1997-1999

UK region	Household income per head, average 1997-99 (UK=100)
London	121
South East	110
East	105
South West	100
Scotland	95
East Midlands	93
North West	93
West Midlands	93
Yorkshire & Humberside	93
North East	89
Wales	88
Northern Ireland	88

Note: Scotland's figure is for 1997 only.

Source: ONS (2002: Tables 12.1, 12.8)

> **Why not competitiveness?**
>
> Much analysis of national, regional and urban policy uses the language of 'competitiveness' as the means of discourse. The objective of economic policy is to improve the 'competitiveness' of the UK, of the region and of the city.
>
> High quality analysis always steers clear of using this term. The reason is that nations or regions do not compete like firms do. The term competition when applied to firms implies winners and losers. For 200 years economic analysis has been trying to show that trade between nations and regions is not a zero-sum game but should be mutually beneficial. If the US economy goes into recession the usual reaction is not to celebrate the problems of a 'competitor' but to worry about the impact on our own economy, given the demand for UK output that emanates from the US. This is not how a firm would react to the problems of one of its 'competitors'. Likewise if one region of the UK economy suffered a reverse all the other regions would be worried about the fallout for them in terms of lower demand.
>
> There is also a practical reason for worrying about the 'cult of competitiveness'. It could lead to bad public policy if it encourages wasteful zero-sum competition between regions, for example in relation to inward investment. An example of this is discussed in Chapter 3.

nearly 60 percentage points in GVA per head between the North East region and London is reduced to a gap in household income per head of just over 30 percentage points. However, very significant disparities remain and there is little impact upon the relative ranking of the regions.

It is of course consistent with the values and analysis of all the political parties that regions, like individuals, should be able to stand on their own two feet. GVA per head is a measure of the economic output of a region; if that region's prosperity is overly reliant on transfer payments from elsewhere, this is unlikely to be regarded as satisfactory by either the recipient or the donor regions. So although transfers are a vitally important component of social policy, economic policy should clearly focus on improving the output of the regions.

The data on household income in Table 2.4 do not take into account differences in the cost of living between the regions. Indeed another of the key deficiencies in the availability of regional statistics is the absence of any regional deflators that could be used to adjust the data to reflect differences in price levels. We can, however, approximate the impact that having such deflators would have on the size of the 'north-south gap'. A report prepared for the Corporation of London made a plausible effort to calculate the difference in the cost of living between the capital and the rest of the country (Gordon *et al* 2002). Key to this effort of course is taking into account differences in housing costs, especially for owner-occupiers. It was estimated that on average the cost of living in London was about 10-12 per cent above the UK average in 2000-01. Applying this estimate to the figures on household income in Table 2.4 would about halve the advantage of London households in terms of income per head to around 9-11 per cent above the UK average. We do not have similar estimates for the disadvantaged regions, but it is plausible to think that the lower cost of living in the North East, for example, would move household income per head in that region somewhat closer to the UK average. A significant gap of somewhere around 15 percentage points in real gross disposable household income per head between London and the North East would be likely to remain, however. This is clearly an area for further work.

Poverty: assigning the right instruments to the right problem

London does have one particular social problem that sets it apart, namely high levels of child poverty. The commonly accepted indicator used in current debates on poverty is a relative measure: 60 per cent of contemporary median household income. A goal of reducing the proportion of people living in households with less than 60 per cent of contemporary median income is widely agreed to be right in principle and has been accepted by the European Union (EU) and the UK Government (Palmer *et al* 2002). It is the measure that the UK Government has chosen to assess progress against its ambitious target to 'reduce the number of children in low income households by at least a quarter by 2004, as a contribution towards the broader target of halving child poverty by 2010 and eradicating it by 2020' (HMT 2002a).

Table 2.5 Regional breakdown of percentage of children living in households with an income of less than 60% (after housing costs) of the national median

GB region	1999-00 excludes self-employed	2000-01 includes self-employed	2001-02 includes self-employed
London	43	41	35
North West	34	32	32
West Midlands	32	37	32
Yorks & Humber	36	29	32
Wales	36	33	31
North East	35	37	31
Scotland	29	30	30
East Midlands	27	29	29
South West	30	27	28
East	25	22	24
South East	25	22	24
Great Britain	**32**	**31**	**30**

Note: Unfortunately the Family Resources Survey (FRS) only started to be collated in Northern Ireland in 2002-03. Figures should be available in the next publication of *Households Below Average Income*, expected in Spring 2004.

Source: DWP (2003: Table 4.8)

Table 2.5 provides the regional breakdown of child poverty rates over the period 1999-2002. There are quite significant regional differentials in child poverty. Children are at a much lower risk of poverty in regions such as the East of England or the South East than in the North East or the North West, but the highest child poverty rate is to be found in London. The figures suggest that levels of child poverty have declined over this period and that regional differences have diminished. It seems, therefore, that the Government's anti-child poverty strategy has been having some success. However, the Government is clearly not yet at a stage where it can be assured that it will meet its target of abolishing child poverty by 2020.

Anti-poverty campaigners have rightly argued that unless the Government commits significant extra resources via such instruments as benefit payments and the child tax credit the target simply cannot be met (Brewer *et al* 2002). However, the Government also needs levels of employment to continue rising and recognises the importance of active labour market policies and other measures in this respect. Bearing in mind the significant regional disparities in employment, a strong regional policy would make a significant contribution to the commitment to eradicate child poverty by 2020.

However, we must be careful to match specific policy instruments to specific problems. The main solution to London's child poverty problem does not lie with regional economic policy instruments. Further significant falls in child poverty are likely to result from tax and benefit policies that channel more resources to families and policies that help heads of households with children (including lone parents) make the transition to stable employment while balancing their caring responsibilities. Regional policy instruments are necessary to address regional economic disparities, and other policy instruments are necessary to deal with other forms of inequality and exclusion.

'Happiness' and quality of life

The relevance of economic performance is that it may be a means to an end. That end is not the consumption of beefburgers, nor the accumulation of television sets, not the vanquishing of some high level of interest rates, but rather the enrichment of mankind's feeling of well-being. Economic things matter only in so far as they make people happier (Oswald 1997).

It is sometimes argued that while the 'North' may not have the prosperity of the 'South', people are on the whole 'happier'. Over the last 20 years there has been a significant growth in the academic literature exploring 'happiness', but despite such themes having some influence in public debate little of the literature has addressed the regional dimension.

Western countries have been experiencing rising real incomes for generations, and the UK approached the 21st century approximately twice as rich as it was in 1960 and three times more affluent than at the end of World War II. Despite this, happiness and satisfaction with life has increased only marginally (Oswald 1997). One reason for this must be that happiness is dependent not only on *absolute* levels of income, but also *relative* levels of income. However, this can only be part of the answer and other factors also fundamentally affect happiness. Richard Layard (2003) surveyed the literature in a series of lectures in 2003 and concluded that, alongside income, the research pointed to six other factors which have a significant impact on people's happiness: work, private life, community, health, freedom and philosophy of life.

Both Layard and Oswald stress that employment is crucial to an individual's happiness and argue that the focus of economic policy should move from economic growth to full employment, which further justifies the emphasis on employment in this report. Lower levels of employment in the 'North' would lead one to infer that the 'South' is likely to be happier than the 'North'. However, we have more direct evidence to draw on.

Self-reported health is strongly related to happiness (Layard 2003). Survey data for 2000-01 on this is contained in Figure 2.2. With the exception of reasonably high levels in Wales, the expected pattern of regional disparities is largely

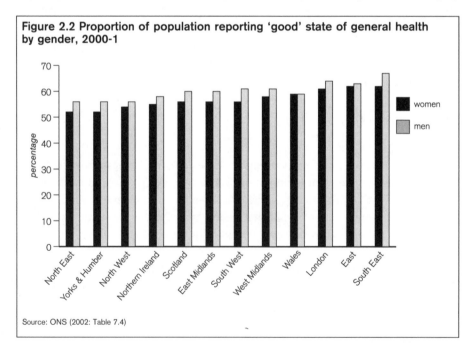

Figure 2.2 Proportion of population reporting 'good' state of general health by gender, 2000-1

Source: ONS (2002: Table 7.4)

confirmed, with people in the 'North' less likely to report a good state of general health than those in the 'South'. Even though objective measures of health are less closely correlated with happiness, it is worth highlighting the extreme regional disparities in the standardised mortality ratio – perhaps the most invidious regional disparity of all (see Figure 2.3). Put bluntly, people in the 'North' die earlier than people in the 'South'.

Mental health is the health variable that is most closely related to happiness (Layard 2003). Table 2.6 provides a regional break-down of rates of depression in England and Wales in 1994-98. It proved impossible to identify regional break-downs for levels of other mental disorders (for example schizophrenia). The data is only available on the old NHS regional office boundaries, and levels of depression are far higher for women than for men. Again the pattern of a broad 'north-south divide' is confirmed. For example, levels of depression for men in the 'Northern and Yorkshire' and 'North West' regions were fully three-fifths higher than for the 'North Thames' region and the absolute differences for women were even higher.

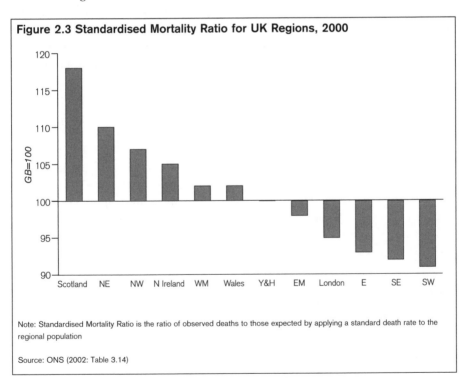

Figure 2.3 Standardised Mortality Ratio for UK Regions, 2000

Note: Standardised Mortality Ratio is the ratio of observed deaths to those expected by applying a standard death rate to the regional population

Source: ONS (2002: Table 3.14)

Table 2.6 Treatment of depression by NHS Regional Office Area, 1994-1998 (rates per 10,000 patients)

English and Welsh regions	Males	Females
Northern and Yorkshire	29.6	70.6
North West	30.4	70.3
Trent	24.7	61.2
Anglia and Oxford	23.7	61.1
South and West	24.1	60.5
Wales	24.0	58.6
West Midlands	21.6	58.6
South Thames	20.6	49.7
North Thames	18.8	46.5
England and Wales	**24.9**	**61.3**

Source: ONS (2002: Table 7.5)

Many issues highlighted as important in the happiness literature are outside the scope of this report (such as personal freedom and philosophy of life). However, it is clear from this brief examination of the topic that there are significant regional disparities in the factors like employment and health that seem to contribute to a more rounded understanding of individual happiness. Those who claim that the 'North' may be poorer but is generally happier would seem to be profoundly misguided.

The environment

In the 21st century, the objective of promoting 'sustainable development' permeates much of the public policy debate. One of the RDAs' five statutory purposes is 'to contribute to sustainable development' and each English region has a sustainable development framework. The Government has established 15 headline indicators designed to provide a review of progress towards achieving sustainable development (ONS/DEFRA 2002). These indicators relate to a range of environmental, social and economic 'outcomes'.

And there's the rub. Because the term 'sustainability' is so widely used and with different meanings by different people and because it has become such an all encompassing concept, it is threatening to lose its usefulness as the basis for thinking about public policy. The Government's headline indicators of sustainable development illustrate the problem. The economic indicators manage to confuse outcomes (GDP per head and employment rates) with one of the drivers of those outcomes (investment). The social indicators are broadly sensible and include child poverty and life expectancy at birth. However, we concentrate here on the environmental indicators, as economic and social indicators are discussed elsewhere.

As Table 2.7 shows, for two of the most important indicators – climate change and air quality – it is not possible to give regional data on a comparable basis to the national headline indicator. For some of these indicators it is not clear that the regional breakdowns are particularly informative and it is very difficult to establish lengthy time series at the regional level that allow for the tracking of progress.

Table 2.7 Headline environment indicators at the regional level

Headline environment indicator	Regional measure comparable with headline indicator
Climate change (emissions of carbon dioxide)	no
Air quality	no
Road traffic	yes
River water quality	yes
Wildlife (regional wild bird population)	partially
Land use (% of new homes built on previously developed land)	yes
Waste	yes

Source: ONS/DEFRA (2002)

Climate change is perhaps the most pressing environmental problem, but carbon emissions can only be attributed to the region in which they take place, which is not necessarily where the 'end user' is located. So the emissions from a power station are allocated to the region where the power station is located, not where the electricity is consumed. Also the capacity of regions to switch to renewable resources such as wind power is obviously constrained by geography as much as by political will. Air quality is one environmental indicator that impacts directly on day-to-day quality of life, but it is not possible to provide regional averages because there are too few sites in some regions where measures are taken.

The data on road traffic use illustrate that London has less of it, but this of course reflects the nature of London as a congested city. Here a measure of change over time as congestion charging makes its impact will be particularly interesting. The data on river water quality and regional wildlife population indices are of significant interest as is the data on volumes of waste produced per head and the proportion that is recycled or composted. The proportion of new homes built on brownfield sites is not quite the same as the RDA key performance indicator: hectares of brownfield land remediated and/or recycled.

One could question whether it matters that for some of the national headline environmental indicators there are poor regional measures. Climate change is clearly an issue primarily addressed at the national or indeed international level, both in terms of analysis and use of policy instruments (though some RDAs such as Yorkshire Forward have done interesting work to see how greenhouse gas emissions at the regional level could be reduced). The environmental issues that matter at the local level are those which directly impact on daily quality of life. These can include air quality and road traffic levels, but also the quality of local public spaces, including public parks, the cleanliness of the streets, noise levels, the efficiency of refuse collection services and so on. These are, of course, some of the major services delivered by local government and illustrate the importance of this tier of government to securing a better environment and quality of life.

Despite the development of these headline indicators and the imposition of statutory duties on regional agencies, it is as yet unclear that the Government has adequately reconciled environmental and economic needs within its overall approach to development. The Government's favoured strategy is to improve productivity whilst using fewer resources. This 'more from less' approach is, according to Porritt (2003) 'a very seductive strategy. It appears to offer an almost pain-free route to a 'cleaner environment' without jeopardising normal economic priorities'. Yet it also presents difficult trade-offs that need to be confronted if the impact of economic activity upon the environment is to be addressed. For example, the imposition of the climate change levy will have had a disproportionate impact on manufacturing industry, which is disproportionately concentrated in the disadvantaged regions.

The development needs of different regions is one area where such issues come into sharp focus. Unfortunately, the data available through the 15 headline indicators, and other government sources, does not allow us to adequately capture the different environmental problems and pressures faced by different regions. As each region pursues its development objectives, so different environmental considerations must be addressed.

For example, London and the South East must address the 'problems of success'. As the Regional Economic Strategy for South East England (SEEDA 2002: 3) argued,

> We cannot build our way out of the congestion problem. We do need urgent investment to provide new transport infrastructure for the region. However, we must also be prepared to tackle the seemingly insatiable demand for road transport.

Such a 'smart growth' approach should be applauded, and, moreover, encouraged in other areas. A more sensitive regional policy would take demand-management policies, such as congestion charging and waste-management, seriously.

Moreover, such a 'smart growth' approach would need to address issues across and between regions as well. For example, the Communities Plan has been characterised as 'bulldozing the North and concreting the South'. Serious consideration must be given to the environmental impacts of the proposed developments across London and the East and South East regions. Moreover, the Communities Plan might only be seen as a short-term solution to *national* development pressures.

A more medium- to long-term approach that recognises the development needs of the northern regions is an imperative. However, the need to boost employment and growth rates within such regions must not privilege economic over environmental concerns. Those within these regions who argue that development on greenbelt land is necessary to secure future regional prosperity need to be challenged. As the 'Happiness' section above demonstrated, economic development in itself does not secure an improving quality of life. So although regions such as the North East require policy mechanisms that help economic growth and promote full employment, a key challenge for regional policy is to do this in a way that has as minimal an impact upon the environment as possible. Demolishing homes in urban areas while building new houses on greenfield sites does not seem sustainable in any sense of the word, even if it might seem imperative as a means of meeting the needs of middle England.

Adequately integrating environmental concerns into development practices presents some tough political challenges. As such, developing a greater regional sensitivity to the environmental pressures generated by development is a key challenge for regional policy. There must be some doubt as to whether the Government, with its over-riding concern with labour productivity, currently has the policy framework or data in place to meet that challenge. Indeed at times it seems that policy makers see the environment in purely instrumental terms: a good environment and quality of life is a means to the end of attracting more economic activity. This is to get matters precisely the wrong way round.

Conclusion: how the market would do it

One obvious question to ask is why normal market mechanisms would not work towards reducing the significant regional economic disparities that we have identified here. It is a question to answer in order to provide a clear justification for public policy to address the problem.

The market should work like this. High costs as the result of tight labour and housing markets in the successful regions should generate incentives for firms and people to relocate to the disadvantaged regions, where the availability of surplus labour and lower costs should prove attractive. In practice there are a number of reasons why such market pressures will not work effectively to even out regional imbalances. However, it is worth emphasising that public policy itself can prevent the market from working. Much attention has been given to factors such as national pay setting that could prevent wages from adjusting in the regions, an issue taken up in Chapter 4. However, an issue less often raised is the possibility that government action to offset the problems faced by successful congested regions will make those regions even more attractive to economic activity. If resources are channelled to build more houses in the successful regions and to improve the transport infrastructure, the very incentives for firms and people to relocate are blunted.

Of course that is exactly how some people would characterise the policies of the current Government in relation to housing and transport. Within a single government department such as the Office of the Deputy Prime Minister there are conflicting pressures to reduce regional disparities and to deliver ambitious aspirations for population and employment growth in the Greater South East. Critics contend that not only is Government policy inconsistent, it runs counter to the one sure way to address the UK's regional economic disparities. This is to 'let the South stew'. Allow congestion and costs to become so disabling in the Greater South East that firms and people are forced to consider relocation.

The usual riposte of course is that firms will relocate abroad, not to the 'North' and that London in particular plays such a vital and irreplaceable role in the national economy, if its development is held back in any way, national economic performance will suffer. At this point the debate usually ends up as a dialogue of the deaf.

Is there any way to reconcile these apparent opposites? The first step is to be clearer about the role that London does play in the UK economy. There is, undoubtedly, some economic activity located in the capital that would be unlikely to be efficiently located anywhere else in the UK. The international financial services located in the City are only the most obvious example. Some business services and elements of the creative industries also probably derive significant benefits from their location in the capital.

However, the unique nature of London's economy should not be over-stated. Figure 2.4 shows the proportions of employment in London that serve different overseas and domestic markets, drawn from employer surveys that have been analysed on behalf of the Corporation of London. About 12 per cent of jobs in London were dependent on markets in the EU and the rest of the world in 1999-2000. By comparison, nearly 29 per cent of jobs served local and borough markets and around 31 per cent served markets across Greater London and the South East. A further 29 per cent of jobs derived from serving markets in the rest of the UK.

So most employment in London is *not* directly associated with serving international markets. If we could measure output in the same way, we could probably show that a higher level of economic activity served international markets, in that value-added is likely to be higher in sectors like international finance. However, Figure 2.5 shows that the relationship between London and the rest of the UK is not one simply of dependence of the latter on the former to generate prosperity. It is also a relationship of *interdependence*, with London reliant on demand in the rest of the country to sustain a high proportion of its jobs. Overall, worrying about whether the

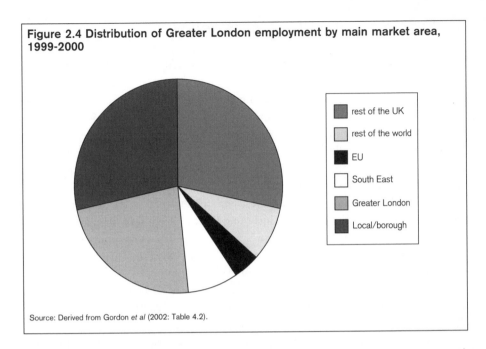

Figure 2.4 Distribution of Greater London employment by main market area, 1999-2000

Legend:
- rest of the UK
- rest of the world
- EU
- South East
- Greater London
- Local/borough

Source: Derived from Gordon *et al* (2002: Table 4.2).

London economy drives the UK or vice-versa is about as pointless as worrying whether it was the chicken or the egg that came first.

As for 'letting the South stew', improvements to the transport infrastructure in the Greater South East, or measures to deliver more homes may well have broad social benefits for people living in those regions. Political reality and social justice demands that these issues are addressed in some fashion. It is reasonable to ask whether the costs of addressing the problems of success should be borne not by the central Exchequer but by the beneficiaries of that success. The realistic political agenda is to find ways of raising revenue within the Greater South East to address the problems of success there. These issues are addressed further in Chapter 7.

3. Employment and regional policy

For many people living in the lagging regions of the UK the proposition that a key problem facing those regions is a lack of jobs would seem so obvious that they might find it hard to believe that this is in fact a matter of serious contention.

It is not in dispute that the proportion of the working age population in employment varies significantly across and within regions. While the employment rate in the UK as a whole in 2003 was higher than in many other OECD countries, some parts of the country suffer from unacceptably low levels of employment. The Government would stress that every region in the UK has an employment rate above the EU average, and that even the lowest employment region has an employment rate higher than most EU countries, including France, Spain and Italy (DfES 1999). However, this does not mean that there is full employment across and within all UK regions, if a definition of over 80 per cent of the working age population in employment is used (Burkitt and Robinson 2001).

Figure 3.1 graphically illustrates regional and local variations in employment, detailing the proportion of the working age population in employment by Travel-To-Work Area (TTWA) across the UK, where the TTWAs approximate relatively self-contained local labour markets where people both live and work. Figure 3.1 shows the broad swathe of TTWAs in the Greater South East, including that part of the South West region along the M4 corridor where employment rates are close to 80 per cent, and the low employment rates in many TTWAs located in the lagging regions. It also shows that this broad 'north-south divide' is overlaid by an *urban-rural* split with relatively high employment rates in areas such as North Yorkshire and generally low employment rates in the major cities, including London.

The most important dispute in regional economic policy debates is over how far these patterns reflect differences in the employment opportunities or jobs available in different localities, or whether they simply reflect the inability or unwillingness of those not in employment to access the jobs that are available. Much of the analysis presented by the Government emphasises the latter supply-side explanation of concentrations of unemployment; the critics prefer the former demand-side explanation focusing on the existence of jobs-gaps across the UK. Without some resolution of this dispute it is hard to see the regional economic policy debate progressing.

The first thing to emphasise about the Government's analysis is that it begs the question as to why we have policy instruments such as Regional Selective Assistance (RSA), one aim of which is to create or preserve jobs in the Assisted Areas. The RDAs are set as one of their key targets the creation or safeguarding of jobs. If there is no shortage of jobs and low employment rates are a supply-side problem there would seem to be a major disjuncture between the analysis and policy.

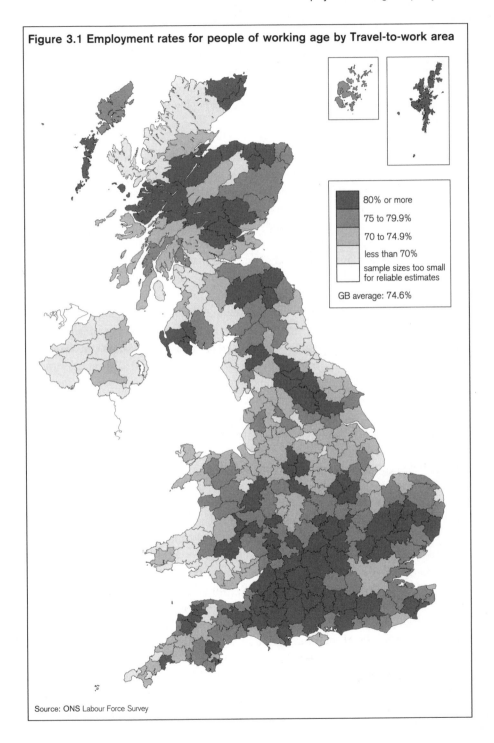

Figure 3.1 Employment rates for people of working age by Travel-to-work area

80% or more

75 to 79.9%

70 to 74.9%

less than 70%

sample sizes too small
for reliable estimates

GB average: 74.6%

Source: ONS Labour Force Survey

What we might refer to as the 'Treasury/Department for Work and Pensions' view was well articulated in a paper published in February 2000.

> Almost without exception, areas of high unemployment lie within easy travelling distance of areas where vacancies are plentiful. This is particularly clear cut in London (HMT/DWP 2000).

This statement with its emphasis on travelling distance does at least appear to back the notion that TTWAs are the appropriate spatial scale to look at employment problems. But critically it juxtaposes two measures, unemployment and vacancies, suggesting an analysis of these is critical to an understanding of the employment problem.

The analysis of unemployment and vacancies does indeed have a long history in economics. At the heart of the analysis is the notion that the level of vacancies can be taken as a proxy for labour demand. The 'Treasury/DWP' argument is then quite straightforward. Following the sharp recession of the early 1980s, by 1986 reported vacancies had recovered to their level in 1979. It follows that labour demand must have recovered to its 1979 level. If unemployment was by 1986 three times higher than in 1979, this had to be a supply-side or structural problem to be dealt with by supply-side measures not measures to increase labour demand. Moreover, vacancies seem pretty evenly spread across the country so that a shortage of jobs cannot explain geographical concentrations of unemployment.

What is interesting is that the Government's critics by and large do not dispute the argument that job vacancies are a good proxy for labour demand. They emphasise that job vacancies are higher in relation to employment or unemployment in the 'South' than in the 'North' and therefore that labour demand is relatively lower in the 'North'. If you compare some measure of the overall level of vacancies with the overall level of non-employment across different areas you can illustrate the existence of 'jobs gaps' in many disadvantaged areas (see for example, Turok and Edge 1999; Erdem and Glyn 2001 for different ways of calculating jobs gaps). Eliminating these jobs gaps requires demand-side measures to increase the numbers of jobs in those areas.

A significant problem in testing these different arguments is the lack of good quality data on the scale of vacancies across the country. For many years we relied on a measure of vacancies reported to Jobcentres, which were then multiplied by a factor of three based on the assumption that the Employment Service received about one-third of all vacancies. This rough-and-ready measure was always controversial; it was suspended in April 2001 after the reliability of the data was increasingly questioned. An enterprise-based survey of job vacancies was adopted as a new series of national statistics in the summer of 2003, with data going back to April 2001 (Machin 2003). Unfortunately there is no regional breakdown of this series available so it will provide no intelligence to help resolve the dispute over the nature of geographical concentrations of low employment (another example of the problem of inadequate regional statistics).

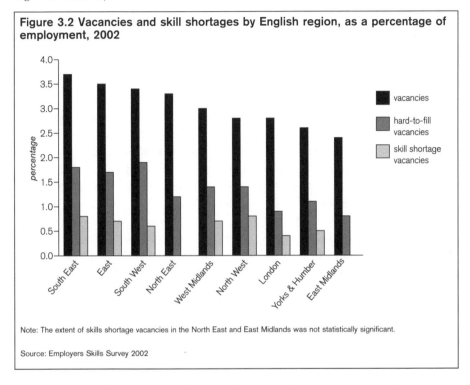

Figure 3.2 Vacancies and skill shortages by English region, as a percentage of employment, 2002

Note: The extent of skills shortage vacancies in the North East and East Midlands was not statistically significant.

Source: Employers Skills Survey 2002

Figure 3.2 is drawn from another employer-based survey that does allow for some regional and local area disaggregation, although unfortunately it was only conducted in England. Interestingly, the 2002 Employers Skills Survey does not yield a straightforward north-south pattern in the scale of overall vacancies, hard-to-fill vacancies or skill shortage vacancies. The South East, East and South West regions had the highest incidence of overall and hard-to-fill vacancies. However, the incidence of vacancies and especially skill shortage vacancies fell sharply in London in 2002 compared with 2001 and 1999. This begs an obvious question: if a modest slowing down in the London economy in 2002 can see skill shortage vacancies so quickly dissipate how binding a problem can such skill shortages be and what exactly is being measured by these indicators?

A more detailed analysis of the 2001 Employers Skills Survey concluded that 'at a broad regional scale a north-south divide is evident' (Green and Owen 2002), a finding that was stronger in 2001 when London was still reporting an above average incidence of overall, hard-to-fill and skill shortage vacancies. The sample of the 2001 survey was boosted to permit analysis of vacancy patterns at the level of the 47 local

Learning and Skills Councils (LSCs) in England. This is not because the LSCs are the best unit for labour market analysis, but rather that they were key customers for this particular analysis. The analysis showed that most of the LSCs with a high incidence of overall, hard-to-fill and skill shortage vacancies lay in the three southern regions and the South West; by contrast all the local LSCs in the North East and Yorkshire and Humber recorded a lower than average incidence of vacancies. However, there was also evidence for an 'urban-rural' divide, with the sharpest contrasts between 'prosperous England' and remoter rural areas on the one hand and areas of existing or past concentrations of mining and manufacturing. It also revealed interesting differences in the type of vacancies that proved hard-to-fill in different parts of England, with three-fifths of the hard-to-fill vacancies in East and Central London in 2001 being for managerial, professional and technical occupations. By contrast in 'remoter rural' areas such as Cumbria over two-thirds were concentrated in the administrative, sales and personal service occupations.

This discussion certainly leaves us with a great deal of scepticism about the utility of the data on vacancies. However, we should perhaps ask questions about how far vacancies really measure the demand for labour as opposed to the turnover in labour that is a constant feature of any working labour market. Turnover in labour is largely driven by voluntary quits as people choose to move on in the labour market. People feel more confident to move on when the economy is doing quite well, which is an important reason why the incidence of vacancies moves with the cycle. The fact that in the 'Treasury/DWP' story vacancies had by 1986 recovered to their 1979 levels illustrates only that with the economic recovery the labour market was registering a healthy rate of turnover once again, not that the absolute demand for labour had returned to its previous levels.

In 2003 another official measure was launched publicly, purporting to offer an indicator of labour demand across the regions and local areas of the UK. The jobs density ratio measures the number of jobs in each region or local area as a proportion of the resident working age population (see Figure 3.3). This measure seems to make little sense at the local authority level, particularly in cities where commuting patterns mean that we should not expect the number of jobs and the number of residents to show much of a match. To learn that in 2001 there were 473 jobs for every 100 residents of working age in Westminster but only 46 jobs per 100 residents in Lewisham is to learn very little, other than confirming that lots of people in Lewisham commute to work in boroughs such as Westminster. At the regional level the new official measure if anything seems to confirm the arguments of those who suggest that there are bigger jobs gaps in the lagging regions, with only 70 jobs for each 100 residents of working age in the North East in 2001 versus 87 in the South East.

Unfortunately, there is as yet no meeting of minds between the Treasury/DWP and its critics over how far geographical concentrations of low employment reflect a

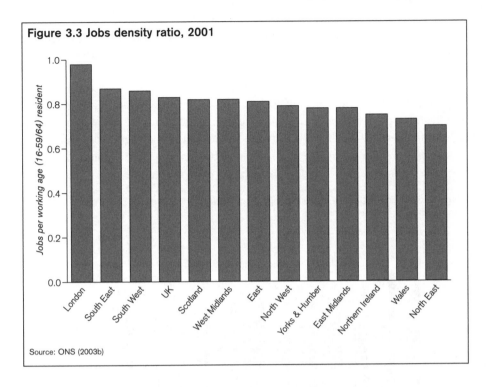

Figure 3.3 Jobs density ratio, 2001

Source: ONS (2003b)

supply-side or a demand-side problem. Intuitively a glance at Figure 3.1 might be more illuminating that any amount of analysis of unemployment and inadequate vacancy data. The official assertion is that 'Almost without exception, areas of high unemployment lie within easy travelling distance of areas where vacancies are plentiful'. Figure 3.1 does not really bear this out. The Hartlepool TTWA with an employment rate of 66.5 per cent in 2001-02 has on its borders the lagging labour markets of Middlesbrough and Stockton (employment rate 66 per cent) and Sunderland and Durham (employment rate 67 per cent). Hartlepool is not within easy travelling distance of anywhere with a tight labour market. The same would go for other groups of TTWAs with low employment rates in, for example, West Wales and the Valleys, industrial West Cumbria or Northern Ireland. In other words many of the traditional Assisted Areas consist of a set of local labour markets next to one another all of which have relatively low employment rates.

The origins of these concentrations of low employment are not hard to find. They stem from the decline of traditional heavy industries, a sectoral decline that was dramatically speeded up in the early 1980s recession, with further restructuring later that decade and into the 1990s. Clearly, these jobs are not going to return. The resulting concentrations of people with redundant skills and often poor formal qualifications can lead to a somewhat dispiriting analysis that such concentrations will be hard to shift. It has been pointed out that in the disadvantaged regions, employment rates are particularly low for the least well qualified (Erdem and Glyn 2001). Of course this is precisely what one would expect to see in conditions of overall low demand for labour, where the effects of general demand deficiency will get concentrated on the lower tiers of the labour market. It does not necessarily follow that such people could not get jobs if the aggregate labour market was not much tighter. In tighter labour markets the employment rates for the less well qualified are much higher: a tight regional labour market will vacuum up many of those that in less tight labour markets face forbiddingly high non-employment rates.

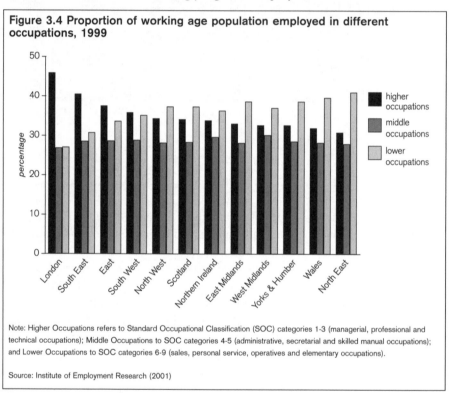

Figure 3.4 Proportion of working age population employed in different occupations, 1999

Note: Higher Occupations refers to Standard Occupational Classification (SOC) categories 1-3 (managerial, professional and technical occupations); Middle Occupations to SOC categories 4-5 (administrative, secretarial and skilled manual occupations); and Lower Occupations to SOC categories 6-9 (sales, personal service, operatives and elementary occupations).

Source: Institute of Employment Research (2001)

We should also not get trapped into thinking that the concentration of unemployment amongst the less well qualified means that we should try to create lots of less well qualified jobs. What is most striking about the disadvantaged regions is their relative lack of well-paid managerial, professional and technical jobs requiring relatively high levels of qualifications (see Figure 3.4). In the North East less than one in three of those in employment in 1999 worked in these higher occupations, compared with nearly half in London. As we will discuss further in Chapter 4 this is why the well qualified in regions such as the North East tend to migrate to the 'South' where more of the 'good' jobs are located. The 'North' needs more good jobs – in business and financial services for example – to retain the well qualified in the region. The existence of such well-paid jobs in traded services such as business services will in turn generate jobs in the generally less well-paid sheltered services such as retailing or the personal services. This seems to be a key reason for the relative success in employment terms of cities such as Leeds and Edinburgh.

Housing and labour mobility

These comments also help clarify what elements of the geographical mobility of labour that we need to concentrate on. The public policy debate had of course been trapped in the 1980s by unhelpful rhetoric about the need for jobseekers to 'get on their bikes' to look for work. Graduates are very mobile across the UK labour market as a whole (Gregg, Machin and Manning 2001). By contrast, unemployed people only appear to move between regions once they find a job; speculative moves in search of work by unemployed people are rare in the UK.

Much of the residential mobility that we observe is unrelated to labour market factors and is over relatively short distances (Dixon 2003) but inter-regional shifts in population can occur as the aggregate outcome of sets of shorter distance moves. For many types of labour there is no doubt that house price differentials between the 'North' and 'South' are an impediment to inter-regional labour mobility. High levels of prosperity and employment in the 'South' are reflected in high levels of housing wealth and high house prices, which then impedes inter-regional mobility. But for most jobseekers the relevant labour market horizon is more local. The relevance of major transport investments to patterns of regional prosperity is explored in Chapter 7, but a focus on local labour markets puts the emphasis on making sure that local public transport connects areas of population with areas of employment. Buses are the most important source of public transport for the less well-off (Grayling 2001).

The Treasury/DWP argument does carry some force in any analysis of concentrations of unemployment in a large metropolitan area like Glasgow or London. To point out the concentrations of non-employment in a borough such as Hackney and to then suggest that the problem is a lack of jobs in Hackney is to misunderstand the way that the labour and housing markets work in a city like London. This has been forcefully argued in a number of important contributions by Ian Gordon (Gordon 1999, Gordon 2003). Many individuals in London have a mix of adverse individual characteristics and face a series of barriers to securing employment. The London housing market operates so as to concentrate these individuals in certain areas where housing is either cheaper or socially provided. The result is concentrations of low employment in these areas.

These concentrations may in turn exacerbate the problems faced by individuals. For example, local schools may be handicapped by having to deal with heavy concentrations of children from disadvantaged backgrounds, with the 'peer group' effect compounding the impact of disadvantage for any one pupil (Feinstein 1998). High concentrations of disadvantaged adolescents may have negative consequences in terms of higher levels of delinquency, with a criminal record one of the biggest barriers to employment (Gregg 2002). Interestingly, this suggests that local people have a good sense of priorities when they report that having opportunities and facilities for children and young people is the aspect of their area that they would most like to see improved (ONS 2003c).

The correct response to these concentrations, however, is not to create jobs in Hackney for Hackney residents, but to equip those residents and break down the barriers they might face so that they can access jobs across the whole of the metropolitan labour market. As Figure 3.1 shows, in London's case this extends even beyond the boundaries of the Greater London Authority.

The supply-side barriers faced by individuals could include:

• a lack of appropriate skills and qualifications or recent work experience

• problems in accessing information about job vacancies or ineffective forms of job search

• employer's recruitment practices that may directly or indirectly discriminate against certain jobseekers

• very specific barriers such as insufficient affordable elder and childcare or poor local transport links

• benefit traps of various kinds that make it difficult for people to make a sustained transition into employment.

This analysis re-emphasises the importance of choosing the right spatial scale at which to analyse labour markets. There is no such thing as the Hackney labour market – daily flows of people across borough boundaries in London and indeed across the whole metropolitan labour market make this notion a nonsense. Special measures to create jobs in a local area like Hackney will induce flows of commuting and population that will negate most of the impact on residents. Hartlepool, however, does constitute a relatively self-contained labour market and one that is far from any other booming labour markets. This insight offers the best chance of trying to reconcile the sharply different characterisations of the employment problem that we have discussed. For the residents of Hackney what is required is a robust overall London labour market allied to supply-side measures to help them access jobs across the whole of the metropolitan labour market. For the residents of Hartlepool what is required are similar supply-side measures to help improve their ability to compete in the labour market combined with policy instruments designed to create more jobs within easy travelling distance.

It might help therefore if the Treasury/DWP modified its position so that it read:

> Some areas of high unemployment lie within easy travelling distance of areas where vacancies are plentiful. This is particularly clear cut in London, but much less obvious elsewhere.

The policy response

Before identifying the precise policy response suggested by this analysis it is worth looking at Table 3.1. This details the trends in employment rates across the UK regions from 1997 to 2002, a period of reasonably steady growth in output and employment. This resulted in an increase in the employment rate in all of the UK's regions. More detailed work by Evans *et al* (2002) has shown that over the period 1995-2000, every area in England benefited from the decline in the proportion of the working age population drawing income related benefits. A rising tide does tend to lift all boats.

Table 3.1 Employment rates for UK nations and regions for 1997 and 2002		
UK nations and regions	*1997*	*2002*
South East	78.4	79.7
South West	77.1	79.0
East	76.6	79.0
East Midlands	75.6	76.4
West Midlands	73.2	74.2
Scotland	71.0	73.7
Yorks and Humberside	71.4	73.3
North West	70.2	72.3
London	69.9	70.5
Wales	68.2	69.8
North East	67.3	68.4
Northern Ireland	67.1	67.7
UK	**73.1**	**74.7**
Source: Labour Force Survey		

This suggests a four-fold policy response to the problem of low employment in the UK's regions:

1   A strong national economy

It goes without saying that a strong national economy is an imperative. Indeed for a region such as London this is much more important than any 'regional policy' *per se*. For the less advantaged regions a rising tide does lift all boats: strong growth in output and employment nationally will be reflected in higher employment in all the regions. Fortunately the macro-economic policy framework that has evolved since 1992 has given the UK a better opportunity than in past decades and arguably in some other countries to maintain the steady growth in output and employment necessary to help resolve regional imbalances.

2   A strong regional policy

A strong national economy is a necessary but not sufficient condition for closing regional disparities in prosperity and crucially those that stem from differences in employment rates. For those regions and sub-regions where there is a concentration of TTWAs with low employment rates, a set of policy instruments is required to help stimulate the demand for labour across the board. The rest of this chapter will explore some of the most visible of those instruments: Regional Selective Assistance and EU Structural Funds. The aim would be to increase labour demand across broad areas of low employment *not* close to tight labour markets. This is *not* the same as *locally* targeted job creation. One issue that needs to be further discussed is whether within the lagging regions, the promotion of employment within specific 'growth areas' is a better tactic than trying to promote employment everywhere. Another tricky issue is whether very localised concentrations of low employment within advantaged regions – such as Thanet in the South East – are best dealt with by trying to generate employment there or in TTWAs close by (for example, Ashford), with improved local transport links connecting the two. These are the kinds of issues best left to local decision-makers.

3   Supply-side measures

Policy instruments designed to help individuals access employment across the local labour market are relevant to all the UK's regions and localities. For cities like London they are the most important set of instruments. They include measures to reduce the numbers of young people leaving the education system with low skills and qualifications and helping more disadvantaged adults to access a range of learning opportunities. Some of these skills related issues are taken up in the Chapter 4. Also relevant are the battery of active labour market policies and tax/benefit reforms designed to help people access employment and to sharpen the incentives to do so.

Those elements of government policy targeted at priority groups such as disabled people, over-50s, lone parents and ethnic minorities will have specific regional impacts as we have seen. Given the concentrations of inactivity due to long-term sickness and disability in the less advantaged regions, measures to improve the employment rates of this group are of particular relevance to tackling regional disparities in prosperity. Some of the strengths and weaknesses of the Government's current approach in this area are addressed in a recent ippr report by Stanley and Regan (2003). The announcement in Budget 2003 to give Jobcentre Plus districts greater flexibility and discretion is very welcome, though it raises questions about the structure of Jobcentre Plus. This UK-wide agency needs to be structured geographically in a way that better fits other regional and local boundaries. Indeed the setting up of Jobcentre Plus was a missed opportunity to align its boundaries with other institutions, such as the Learning and Skills Councils in England.

4   Measures to reduce residential segregation and the links between segregation and disadvantage

The analysis presented in this report does not suggest a focus only on the efficiency with which labour markets function. We have seen that the way that housing markets function leads to concentrations of non-employment and associated deprivation that may compound the problems faced by disadvantaged jobseeekers. There is clearly an agenda here for housing policy: housing authorities have to take seriously the objective of trying as far as possible to create mixed neighbourhoods, mixed by tenure, ethnicity, class and educational background. But there is also an agenda for other areas of social policy especially in relation to children and adolescents. The evidence for the adverse outcomes that result from heavily segregated schools is perhaps clearer than anywhere else. The appropriate policy response is to look at all those issues relating to catchment areas and to formal and informal methods of selection that result in polarised intakes. 'No selection and less polarisation under Labour' might be a mantra that it is time to resurrect. There is an important set of supply-side policies that pose real challenges for middle England.

A strong regional policy: creating jobs in the regions

1   Regional Selective Assistance

For those regions and sub-regions where there is a concentration of TTWAs with low employment rates, what set of policy instruments can be used to help stimulate the demand for labour across the board? The Government already possesses one policy tool that has the aim of creating or safeguarding jobs within the disadvantaged regions. Regional Selective Assistance (RSA), according to Harvey Armstrong 'remains the most important of the *national* regional policy instruments in Britain. Alongside the European Union's Structural Funds programmes, it forms the backbone of regional policy in Britain' (Armstrong 2001, original emphasis).

RSA is a discretionary grant awarded to projects within Assisted Areas where capital expenditure exceeds £500,000, and where it can be proven that the expenditure would not have happened without the provision of grant funding. For projects where the capital expenditure is lower than £500,000, another discretionary scheme, the Enterprise Grant Scheme, was established in 2000 and is run by the Small Business Service. In England, RSA grants of under £2 million are administered by the RDAs, but for grants of over £2 million the DTI has retained control. RSA grants can be provided to: establish a new business; expand, modernise and/or rationalise an existing business; set up research and development facilities; or enable businesses to take the next step from development to production (DTI 2003). The Government has since 1998 emphasised the need for RSA to support 'high quality, knowledge-based' projects in line with its productivity agenda, but in practice as the National Audit Office (NAO) (2003) noted, in regions such as the North East, securing jobs has continued to be the main objective for the scheme.

RSA has had somewhat of a chequered history in meeting its three objectives of attracting or retaining internationally mobile investment, improving the competitiveness of firms in disadvantaged areas, and creating or safeguarding employment. The NAO (2003) argued that RSA had a poor record in terms of promoting productivity and 'competitiveness', though to be fair these were not the objectives of the scheme over the periods when it has been subject to evaluation. However, the NAO also acknowledged that RSA had made important contributions to the attraction of mobile international investment and, importantly, increasing levels of employment in Assisted Areas.

It is unfortunate that the media seized upon the NAO report's argument that the levels of employment created or secured by RSA had been less than expected. Three comments could be made in relation to this observation.

First, it has been observed by commentators such as Armstrong (2003) that RSA suffers from the problem of 'asymmetric evaluation'. Other policies that are 'flavour of the month' such as business clusters have not been subjected to the same robust evaluations as RSA has. The NAO explicitly acknowledged this, noting that 'the depth and frequency of evaluations [of RSA] compared well with other Departmental schemes and with evaluation practices for similar schemes run by other countries' (NAO 2003, para 16)

Second, it could be argued that RSA remains a fairly cost-effective job-creation tool. Indeed, both Armstrong (2001) and Wren (2002) argue that this cost-effectiveness has significantly improved in recent years, not least because regional assistance has operated on a selective rather than an automatic basis since the 1980s. The most recently published DTI evaluation of RSA, covering the period 1991-1995, supported this conclusion. An Arup report indicated that RSA grants made during this period created or safeguarded 40,000 net additional permanent job equivalents, at a net cost per job of £17,500 in 1995 terms (Arup Economics and Planning 2000). The NAO argued that the evaluation over-estimated the additional net jobs created and therefore underestimated the net cost per job. However, even their revised estimates of 21,000 extra jobs at a net cost per net job of nearly £21,000 (at 2002 prices) over 1991-1995 represented much needed jobs in areas of high unemployment.

Finally, portrayals of RSA as a grant which has 'wasted millions' (Blitz and Chung 2003) fails to appreciate the necessity of an instrument that is geared towards generating jobs in the UK's lagging regions. In the absence of other instruments geared to this end, the abandonment of RSA or an equivalent scheme would send all the wrong signals. So rather than trying to dismantle RSA, we should concentrate on enhancing the effectiveness of this important policy tool within the regions that require a stimulation to labour demand.

There are several ways in which RSA itself or any revised instrument that might replace RSA (and Enterprise Grants) could be re-structured to enhance its effectiveness.

- We need to return to a more rational basis for defining the Assisted Areas where RSA would be available

- More assistance should be channelled to service industries than at present

- Less RSA should be used to support big inward investment projects as opposed to indigenous enterprises

- Consideration should be given to increasing the amount of spending allocated to RSA

Defining the Assisted Areas

The decision was made in 2000 to use wards rather than TTWAs to define the boundaries for the Assisted Areas. The subsequent creation of a patchwork of small areas eligible for assistance was a quite deliberate political decision to spread the regional jam thinly. However, wards are an inappropriate spatial scale at which to address the issue of creating employment. As Gordon (1999) has emphasised trying to create employment in a small geographical area is like 'targeting a leaky bucket': most of the jobs created will not necessarily go to local residents. The boundaries used must more adequately reflect the spatial pattern of low employment areas if RSA is to meet its job-creation objective more effectively. TTWA boundaries will themselves need to be adjusted following the 2001 Census, but they remain the best available way of mapping spatial variations in employment. Most critically we need to re-concentrate effort on those regions and sub-regions where there is a concentration of TTWAs with low employment rates.

By being targeted at the ward level, RSA grants are often focused on the areas of highest unemployment and deprivation, potentially excluding nearby areas of potential employment growth. By redrawing the map along TTWA lines, this 'patchy' coverage would be reduced, and the Assisted Area boundaries would more often include areas more likely to attract new employment. Indeed having a smaller number of Assisted Areas each drawn with somewhat wider boundaries would better fit the Government's own emphasis on encouraging wider travel-to-work horizons and allow for some concentration of effort. The corollary of course is that the patchwork quilt of wards with Assisted Area status outside of the disadvantaged regions would disappear. But isolated wards in London do not need instruments to promote job creation; their residents need supply-side measures designed to help them access jobs across the metropolitan labour market alongside measures to promote physical regeneration. In short they need urban policy and welfare-to-work initiatives, not regional policy.

Redressing the manufacturing bias

The NAO highlighted that the majority of RSA grants are allocated to the manufacturing sector (about 90 per cent of the value of grant offered over the period 1994-2002). The manufacturing sector is important and should not be neglected. But as a recent ippr report (Brooks and Robinson 2003) argued, it is a sector that is likely to continue to decline as a proportion of total output and employment. For those regions still disproportionately dependent on manufacturing, a critical objective is to help them diversify their employment base by attracting a higher proportion of 'non-local' or traded services including, for example, business services. RSA should, therefore, be more aggressively marketed to service sector companies. More emphasis should also be placed on the use of RSA to support Research and Development and other forms of innovative activity that may not involve really big programmes of capital spending.

Fewer prestige inward investment projects

One of the most important ways of making RSA more cost-effective would be to use it less for attracting large 'prestige' inward investment projects and to steer it more firmly to supporting the creation and expansion of smaller indigenous enterprises. The NAO report pointed out that 53 per cent of the value of grant awarded over the period 1992-2002 went to foreign owned companies. Furthermore, Foreign Direct

Investment (FDI) is disproportionately concentrated in the Greater South East especially for non-manufacturing projects. The NAO report also hinted at the possibility of foreign-owned firms playing off different agencies against one another. One case study was quoted of a grant being paid to retain an American-owned plant in the West Midlands in the face of enticements from Northern France *and* the National Assembly for Wales and the Welsh Development Agency. That kind of poaching within the UK is exactly the form of damaging zero-sum competition the media should really pick up on. The DTI needs to improve its regulation of pointless zero-sum competition and understand better its control of this aspect of RSA.

In any case, the importance of incentives such as RSA in relation to FDI is continually being re-appraised. Hubert and Pain (2002) investigated the impact of fiscal incentives on the location of FDI by German firms in Europe. Perhaps unsurprisingly, they found that the generosity of the corporate tax regime was associated with higher FDI, and thus a rise in corporate tax rates would act to deter inward investment. In addition, the level of general government fixed investment had an important positive effect, perhaps reflecting infrastructure investment. However, expenditure on government subsidies was found to be unrelated to levels of FDI. The policy conclusion from this work seemed clear: subsidies designed to attract FDI should either be redirected to infrastructure investments or scrapped with a corresponding reduction in corporate tax rates.

More resources for RSA?

One key outstanding issue is whether there should be a significant increase in spending on RSA. This has certainly been argued for by many engaged in regional policy debates (for example, Regional Studies Association 2001). Through a combination of reductions in regional assistance and the progressive tightening of eligibility criteria, spending on RSA is in real terms now less than one-tenth of what it was 20 years ago (Wren 2002). It is also significantly lower on a per capita basis in the lagging English regions than in Scotland, Wales and Northern Ireland as Figure 3.5 shows. There is thus a reasonably good case for boosting the overall RSA budget, with two aims: to increase funding in the lagging English regions and to increase funding for service sector enterprises without reducing funding for manufacturing. Whether this is really the best use of available resources is discussed further below.

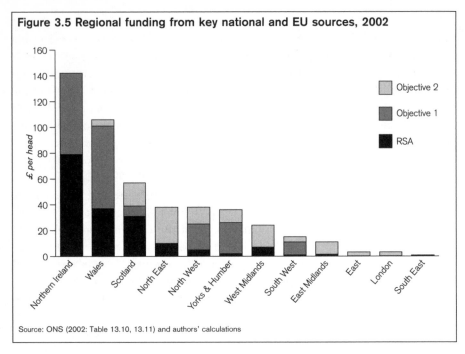

Figure 3.5 Regional funding from key national and EU sources, 2002

Source: ONS (2002: Table 13.10, 13.11) and authors' calculations

2   EU Structural Funds

Several of the UK's disadvantaged regions have been the recipients of EU Structural Funds: indeed as Figure 3.5 shows these funds have been of significantly greater importance to most of those regions than RSA. Objective 1 funding is targeted at regions where GDP per head is less than 75 per cent of the EU-15 average. Over the period 2000-06 it will benefit Cornwall, Merseyside, South Yorkshire and West Wales and the Valleys, with transitional funding for areas where funding from the previous round has come to an end, specifically Northern Ireland and the Highlands and Islands of Scotland. There is also additional special provision for Northern Ireland to support the peace process. Objective 2 funding is aimed at regions suffering from major structural problems and as Figure 3.5 shows is particularly important for low employment regions such as the North East where it dwarfs the RSA budget. There is also an Objective 3 pot aimed at supporting education, training and employment policies.

An important joint consultation paper from the Treasury, DTI and ODPM *A Modern Regional Policy for the United Kingdom* (2003) accepted that the eastward expansion of the EU after 2006 was likely to cut dramatically the Structural Funds available to the current EU member states' poorest regions. Most EU Structural Funds will – rightly – flow to regions in Eastern Europe that will have levels of GDP per head below 75 per cent of the EU-25 average. To support this shift in Structural Funds, as the UK government does, is consistent with the aims of a pro-European centre-left government. Yet even if this is accepted, there is still the question of how the pressing needs of the UK's lagging regions can be addressed. After 2006 perhaps only Cornwall will remain eligible for Objective 1 status. The loss of the resources provided by this other major instrument of regional policy within the UK – along with RSA – could have serious implications for the lagging regions.

To address this issue, the Government has proposed a 're-nationalisation' of regional policy within the existing higher income member states. Specifically this would be a re-nationalisation of Objective 2 funding. In essence the UK Government wants to see policy separated from funding – regional policy would remain an area of competence for the EU Commission. Under a 'EU Framework for Devolved Regional Policy' richer member states with the financial and institutional strength to do so would resource regional policy domestically, whilst supporting EU Framework objectives. The Government has guaranteed that domestic regional funding would be increased. However, it should be noted that this guarantee does not mean a continuation of the existing level of receipts – rather it covers those receipts that UK regions might have been eligible for if the current allocation criteria were applied across an enlarged EU.

Given the emphasis we have given to the need to tackle low levels of employment in the disadvantaged regions there is an obvious way to 're-nationalise' regional policy in a manner that would continue to emphasise the Government's commitment to the EU's agenda. The Lisbon summit in 2000 had a twin focus on employment and productivity. However, its clearest headline goal was the objective of ensuring that all parts of the EU meet a target of at least 70 per cent of the adult workforce in employment by 2010. One way of emphasising the UK's commitment to this objective would be to concentrate additional UK government resources on those TTWAs in the disadvantaged regions with employment rates at or below 70 per cent. This would provide a useful 'floor target' for regional policy. The Assisted Areas map would be re-drawn in the manner suggested above.

It is not, however, necessarily the case that the additional UK government spending designed to compensate for the withdrawal of EU Structural Funds would only go on instruments such as RSA. It might well be more effective to use the funding for regional or local transport improvements for example, or for additional active labour market programmes. The most effective use of additional resources would be best left to local and regional agencies.

Conclusion

An important explanation for regional disparities in prosperity is the low employment rates in the less advantaged regions of the UK. The nature of the employment problem, however, is different across labour markets. For the residents of deprived areas within otherwise prosperous cities, what is required are supply side measures to help them access jobs across the whole of the metropolitan labour market. For the large set of Travel-To-Work Areas in the disadvantaged regions where employment rates are uniformly low, what is required are similar supply-side measures to help people improve their ability to compete in the labour market, combined with policy instruments designed to create more jobs within easy travelling distance.

Addressing low employment rates requires a four-fold policy response:

- A strong national economy

- A strong regional policy

- Supply side measures

- Measures to reduce residential segregation and the links between segregation and disadvantage

The desirable re-focusing of EU Structural Funds after enlargement in 2006 offers the opportunity to re-invigorate regional policy in the UK. The Assisted Areas map should be re-drawn and regional instruments such as RSA concentrated to focus on the set of TTWAs in the disadvantaged regions with employment rates at or below the 70 per cent 'floor' identified by the Lisbon process. More resources would be made available, though not only through Regional Selective Assistance. RSA itself needs to be rebalanced so it focuses less on big inward investment projects and more on traded services.

4. The regional skills, education and training agenda

One of the important advantages of giving employment as much consideration as productivity in the regional policy agenda is that it allows for a much more detailed discussion of the role of skills, education and training to that agenda. Indeed it allows one to immediately clarify that different elements of education and training policy are likely to be relevant to employment on the one hand and to productivity on the other. The current policy debate is often confused on this point, with government priorities in relation to the attainment of basic skills and lower level qualifications for example, sold in official policy documents in relation to their contribution to productivity, when their contribution to employment is actually much more obvious. To reiterate the point, documents like *Productivity 3* remove emphasise the role of skills as one of the drivers of productivity, but do not emphasise the role of education and training as one of the drivers of employability.

There are other confusions in the debate. The term 'workforce development' is used loosely to describe all adult education and training activity outside of higher education. It thus confuses the training that firms undertake with the education and training that individuals undertake. This distinction is of vital importance in policy terms. Policies aimed at individuals are likely to differ significantly from policies aimed at firms; if the two are confused, the result could be confusing policies. Firms undertake training as part of their wider plans for the development of their workforce to meet their core business objectives; the demand for training is derived from those objectives. The economic motivation for individuals to undertake their own learning activities is to secure progression in the labour market and higher lifetime earnings. For the individual securing this progression may mean leaving their current employer, the point being that the motivations of firms and of individuals may not always or indeed often converge.

Most public funding of education and training follows the individual learner, covering all or part of the direct costs of courses at a range of institutions and sometimes helping with the indirect costs (like materials or transport) and with maintenance too. Much more modest sums go towards policy instruments aimed specifically at employers. This is clearly right in principle. Public policy should be aimed first and foremost at lowering those barriers, including financial, that prevent individuals from obtaining the qualifications and skills they need to progress. Public policy should avoid subsidising firms to do what they should be doing anyway in terms of developing their workforce to meet their business objectives. Unfortunately, the public policy debate has been blown off course by – largely unsubstantiated – arguments that the learning chosen by individuals somehow does not fit the requirements of employers, leading to widespread skill shortages, with the additional argument that planning bodies could do a better job of matching the two.

This debate is in turn linked to the discussions about the right spatial scale at which to organise post-compulsory education and training policy in England. From April 2003 two pilot schemes were launched to give some RDAs a leading role in the management and co-ordination of Business Links, and also responsibilities for co-managing with local Learning and Skills Councils (LSCs) funding for post-19 education and training outside of higher education. This would involve 'pooling' the RDAs' very modest skills budgets (largely aimed directly at employers) with the much bigger budgets for education and training held by the local LSCs (aimed at individuals). These developments were seen, rightly, as another indication of the relative influence of the RDAs on policy makers at the Treasury, with the suspicion that this 'pooling' could be the precursor to the RDAs taking over responsibility entirely for the funding of post-19 education and training outside of Higher Education. However, the Skills White Paper (DfES 2003a) signalled a much more modest agenda of the RDAs leading on the establishment of Regional Skills Partnerships which would be unlikely to control budgets and therefore have much power.

From September 2002 a range of Employer Training Pilots has also been underway in a number of local LSC areas to test out a range of incentives to employers to release staff to undertake learning aimed at achieving better basic skills and qualifications at level 2. These pilots are well targeted at helping existing employees to obtain the skills and qualifications likely to improve their employability. The results of a thorough evaluation of these pilots will become available from 2004. It will be a good test of the model of evidence-based policy making to see if the Government can wait that long to see how well the different incentives have worked in practice before launching any policy nationwide.

We will return to some of these important policy agendas later in the chapter, but first it is important to set out how the regions vary in terms of the qualifications and skills of their workforces. This will be the result both of the outputs of the education and training systems *within* each region and, as importantly, patterns of selective migration of labour *between* the regions.

How the regions compare

Generally qualifications are used as a proxy for skills in much analysis and policy debate, for the simple reason that the holding of qualifications is something that we can more easily measure. Overall there is a fairly clear 'north-south gap' across the *English* regions in terms of the stock of qualifications held by people of working age (Figure 4.1). In particular London and the South East have significantly higher proportions of the working age population with higher education (level 4+) qualifications and lower proportions of the population with no qualifications. The three northern English regions and the Midlands regions have fewer graduates and more unqualified people.

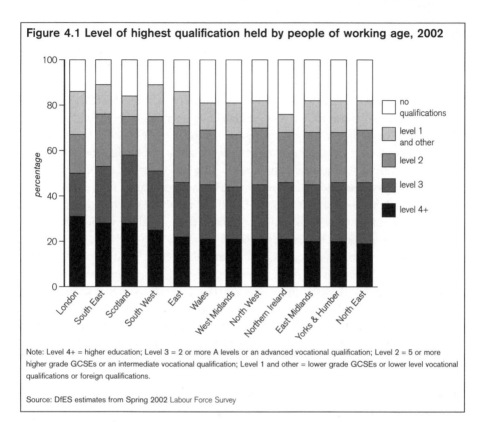

Figure 4.1 Level of highest qualification held by people of working age, 2002

Note: Level 4+ = higher education; Level 3 = 2 or more A levels or an advanced vocational qualification; Level 2 = 5 or more higher grade GCSEs or an intermediate vocational qualification; Level 1 and other = lower grade GCSEs or lower level vocational qualifications or foreign qualifications.

Source: DfES estimates from Spring 2002 Labour Force Survey

It is sometimes wrongly stated that London has a disproportionate number of people with 'low' and no qualifications. London indeed has the highest proportion of people of working age with *level 1* and *other* qualifications. In this context level 1 qualifications include lower grade GCSEs and CSEs and lower level vocational qualifications; but the 'other' qualifications category includes foreign qualifications that cannot be matched to the UK qualifications framework. London's relatively high proportion of people with other qualifications is thus likely to reflect its high migrant population.

However, the pattern is significantly complicated by consideration of the other nations of the UK. Scotland also has a relatively high proportion of graduates in its working age population, though it has greater numbers of unqualified people too. Wales and Northern Ireland are similar to the less advantaged English regions in terms of the proportions with qualifications at level 4 and above, but Northern Ireland has a bigger proportion of the working age population lacking any qualifications: about one quarter in 2002.

So whether the link is with productivity and/or employment, there is certainly a good case for saying that the qualifications of the working age population in the different nations and regions of the UK reflect, albeit imperfectly, different patterns of prosperity. However, as with all the debates over the role of education and training in relation to aggregate economic outcomes, the key issue is disentangling cause and effect. It is certainly plausible to argue that high value added economic activity will be attracted to regions with a well-qualified workforce; that the availability of skilled labour will help foster innovation and facilitate investment and that the well qualified will generally have higher labour force participation rates. On the other hand, the presence of well paid jobs demanding significant skills and qualifications will also attract those with high educational attainment and where such jobs are in short supply in a region the well qualified may well leave. This was recognised in the *Productivity 3* report which worried about regions being 'vulnerable to virtuous and vicious circles', with the lagging regions finding it difficult to retain highly skilled workers in the absence of sufficient good employment opportunities.

If we look at patterns of educational attainment at the end of compulsory schooling, Scotland is recorded as having the highest proportion of 16 year olds achieving 5 or more higher grade GCSE/SCEs (in summer 2001) followed by Northern Ireland (Table 4.1). The South East, East and South West regions also had high proportions with a good batch of higher grade GCSEs, but London was more similar to the Midlands and the North West, although the North East and Yorkshire and Humber had the lowest proportions. Wales had the highest proportion with no graded results.

Table 4.1 Educational attainment at 16

	percentage of pupils achieving 5+ GCSEs at A-C by summer 2001	percentage with no graded results
Scotland	59.3	4.7
Northern Ireland	56.7	4.5
South East	55.5	5.0
South West	54.6	4.6
East	54.0	4.6
Wales	49.8	7.9
East Midlands	49.1	5.5
London	48.6	5.5
North West	48.0	5.7
West Midlands	47.4	5.7
Yorkshire and Humber	44.4	6.2
North East	43.9	6.5

Source: DfES; National Assembly for Wales; Scottish Executive; Northern Ireland Department of Education

There are two points to make about this pattern of results. First, we should want to question the comparability of the data for the four nations of the UK where qualifications systems do differ (though if it is hard to compare across the nations of the UK this might also counsel caution about easy comparisons of qualifications between the UK and other countries).

Second, the results should remind us that a range of background factors such as social class and parental education and experience of child poverty are major determinants of educational attainment. It could be argued that given its relatively high levels of child poverty and all the challenges posed by such a diverse pupil base, the results posted by London's schools are creditable (Johnson 2003). Although 'value-added' analysis of educational attainment is in its relative infancy and is much contested, the finding reported in the Cabinet Office Strategy Unit Analytical Report on London (Cabinet Office 2003a) that London's schools appear to add more value to individual pupil performance between Key Stage 3 and GCSE is very interesting. This same analysis also suggested that North East schools added less value. Relatively high levels of child poverty, a significantly higher proportion of parents from lower social class backgrounds and without higher education will help explain the position of the North East at the bottom of Table 4.1, but the relatively poor performance of North East schools may also be a factor.

There is thus the potential of a further vicious circle here: less advantaged regions, where fewer parents have experience of higher education and more children experience poverty, will have lower levels of educational attainment. Then those young people who do attain good qualifications may migrate out of the region in the absence of enough good jobs locally. Both processes will help explain the correlation between economic success and the attainment of qualifications.

The proportion of 16 year olds staying on in full-time education or in government supported training in 1999-2000 was significantly higher in Scotland, but varies only modestly across the English regions (Table 4.2). This, however, hides a pattern that regions with high proportions going into full-time education tend to have lower proportions going into training and vice-versa, with the three most advantaged English regions having higher staying-on rates in full-time education. These patterns are partly related to differences in industrial structure and partly to differences in attainment at 16, with a solid batch of GCSE results a good predictor of staying on in full-time education. However, even adjusting for GCSE results, strong regional differences in staying on rates in full-time education have persisted for many years (Payne 1998, 2001). Using data pooled from the Youth Cohort Study for 1988-1995 and controlling for a range of background factors, Payne (1998) found the odds of staying on were highest in London and the South East. Payne (2001) emphasised that the links between the local labour market, local social and economic conditions, local cultural norms and local structures of education and training provision need to be much better understood if geographical inequalities in educational participation were to be tackled.

There is plenty of evidence for the selective out-migration of the better qualified from the lagging English regions. Figure 4.2 provides a snapshot based on data from

Table 4.2 16 year olds participating in post-compulsory education and government-supported training, 1999-2000

| | In further education[1] | | | Government- | All in full-time |
	at school[2]	full-time	part-time	supported training (GST)[3]	education and GST[3,4]
Scotland	69.0	11.7	8.9	9.0	89.8
South West	39.0	35.1	5.6	7.1	80.6
South East	39.8	35.4	4.2	5.4	80.2
East	40.8	34.0	5.2	6.0	80.2
London	40.3	34.6	4.6	4.2	78.9
Wales	37.9	33.3	5.7	7.1	78.3
East Midlands	37.7	31.7	8.8	9.2	78.0
North West	24.6	42.5	6.8	11.1	77.1
West Midlands	31.9	37.0	7.6	8.8	76.8
Yorks & Humber	30.9	35.0	9.1	11.6	76.7
North East	26.3	37.5	8.7	not available	not available
Northern Ireland	47.8	28.7	8.7	not available	not available
United Kingdom	38.5	33.6	6.6	8.3	79.6

Notes:

1 students on courses outside of school but below higher education level, including sixth form colleges in England and a small element of further education in higher education institutions in England and Scotland.

2 residence-based.

3 GST figures for Tees Valley, and therefore the North East, were not available at the time of data collection. Figures in the UK row refer to GB.

4 Figures for England exclude overlap between full-time education and government-supported training.

Source: ONS (2002: Table 4.8)

the Labour Force Survey for 2000-02 and shows the five northern and midlands regions losing people with post-school qualifications to the southern regions, though Scotland and Wales also show up as modest net importers of the better qualified. Highly qualified people who leave the less advantaged English regions are, unsurprisingly, acting quite rationally. For example, there is evidence that graduates from North East universities that leave the region after graduation do better than those who choose to remain (Belt *et al* 2002). This finding is based on data on the first destinations of graduates, but the drifting away of the better qualified is likely to be a cumulative affair. Public agencies in regions such as the North East give great attention to graduate retention programmes, but in the absence of a sufficient supply of 'good' jobs to retain the highly qualified, such programmes face an uphill struggle.

The data on the qualifications held by young people and the working age population reflect wholly or largely the outputs of the formal, publicly funded, education and training system, from the schools and further and higher education. Firms also provide more specific job-related training, occasionally including provision purchased from outside the firm. Figure 4.3 shows the standard measure drawn from the Labour Force Survey of the percentage of male and female employees of working

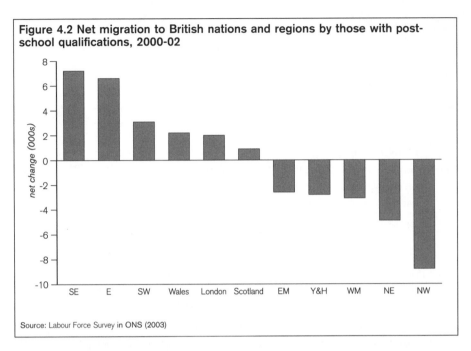

Figure 4.2 Net migration to British nations and regions by those with post-school qualifications, 2000-02

Source: Labour Force Survey in ONS (2003)

age receiving any job-related training in the previous four weeks. It shows no significant variation by region and what variations there are will almost certainly be explained by differences in industrial structure.

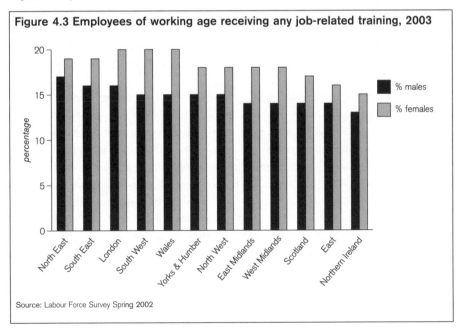

Figure 4.3 Employees of working age receiving any job-related training, 2003

Source: Labour Force Survey Spring 2002

Policy implications

Importantly then for public policy, the significant regional variations in workforce qualifications evident in Figure 4.1 are:

● *not* a consequence of significant differences in the incidence of job-related training

● partly a consequence of differences in educational attainment evident at 16 and staying on rates in full-time education post-16; but these differences are themselves at least in part explained by differences in social and economic background factors between the regions

● partly a consequence of the selective out-migration of the better qualified to the more prosperous regions where a higher proportion of better jobs is on offer

The implications for public policy are to a certain extent clear. Policies to incentivise (or in a statutory framework, force) firms to offer more job-related training may be of little relevance as a tool of regional policy, as firms in the disadvantaged regions do *not* appear to train less than those in the advantaged regions. There will be widespread support for the objective of continuing to improve the outcomes of the publicly funded education and training system, to encourage better attainment at 16 and to improve staying-on rates and attainment post-16. In part this relies on the education system being able to compensate for some of the adverse social and economic background factors that help to explain poor attainment. However, if the result is a better qualified supply of labour in a region like the North East, there is no reason to think that this might not simply translate into a higher rate of selective out-migration of the well qualified to more prosperous regions in the absence of policies that bring more highly skilled jobs to the North East.

The Government has a number of key targets to increase the proportion of young people and of adults attaining qualifications at level 2 and to reduce the number of adults with poor basic skills. These are clearly of relevance to attempts to increase labour force participation, there being strong evidence that attainment at around this level is associated with a significantly higher probability of being in employment (Robinson and Oppenheim 1999). These policies are often misleadingly sold as part of the productivity agenda, but as they are broadly the right policies perhaps we should not get too upset by this. The high profile target for 50 per cent of each cohort to enter higher education by age 30 is more controversial, there having been no labour market justification offered for such an expansion (Piatt and Robinson 2001). This target was also launched without anyone at the time knowing what the rate of enrolment on this measure was and we still lack data on this measure by region. Given the evidence for selective out-migration especially of graduates and given low employment rates in the less advantaged regions, for them the focus on attainment of basic skills and level 2 qualifications is surely the right priority.

The question then arises as to which specific policy instruments and which structures of funding and delivery should different regions and local areas have to meet their objectives for improving the attainment of skills and qualifications, especially at lower levels.

The debate over whether to 'regionalise' the local Learning and Skills Councils' budgets for adult education and training is driven by the notion that the result would be a better match between the skills of the workforce and the demands of employers through the operation of some form of planning mechanism. This aspiration is embodied in the Frameworks for Regional Employment and Skills Action (FRESAs) drawn up by the RDAs in consultation with other stakeholders. In fact such documents tend to be very general in nature, with little attention to priority setting: the London FRESA identifies sectors for priority action that make up 95 per cent of employment in the capital.

The debate also treats subliminally the key issue involved in any attempt to give greater priority to 'planning'. Currently, public funding follows the adult learner, creating a quasi-market where the individual reads the signals from the labour market and chooses a course from a provider that would best secure individual progression. Good quality information and guidance, a competitive provider network and a range of actions to tackle barriers facing individual learners are necessary to make such a quasi-market work effectively. If the criticism of this quasi-market is that the existence of widespread skill shortages shows that too many individuals are making the 'wrong' decisions, the alternative would presumably involve the planners constraining those choices and encouraging individuals to make different decisions. This boils down to a belief that the planners could make better decisions than adults could about their own individual learning. This would seem peculiar logic: 18 year olds are assumed to be able to take their own informed decisions in relation to higher education; why are mature adults assumed not to be able to take their own informed decisions in relation to further education and training?

The debate over regionalisation is therefore to a certain extent a bit of a red herring. The real issue is whether we want to continue to empower individuals to make their own informed choices or whether we want to 'plan' to meet the 'needs' of the labour market as identified by bodies such as the RDAs. As most jobseekers are reading their signals from the local labour market and given that information and guidance are best provided and practical barriers to learning best tackled at a local level, and it is generally desirable to avoid unnecessary administrative upheaval, the current arrangements might be best left alone. The Government's current emphasis on establishing entitlements for individuals to access education and training if they lack skill and qualifications should imply that the funding continues to follow the learner.

But in this case the RDAs would simply be the conduit through which funding flowed as with the local LSCs now, but with little discretion over that funding. This would seem to be a pointless administrative upheaval. It is also worth noting that if the response of the Government to the Employer Training Pilots leads to a statutory framework for employer-provided training, this would, as a measure of labour market regulation, probably have to be introduced on a UK wide basis. This could raise issues in relation to the UK's devolved governance arrangements of far greater importance than the respective roles of RDAs and local LSCs in England.

The RDAs should have a different objective from trying to make better choices over learning on behalf of individual adults. They should concentrate on offering more effective help directly to employers to develop their workforces in the light of their wider business needs. As Business Links are designed to provide various forms of assistance to firms in developing a better understanding of their business needs, joining up Business Links with the modest budgets held by RDAs to help firms meet their training needs sounds like a more helpful step, if indeed Business Links are regarded as effective. The role of the (UK-wide) Sector Skills Councils would also need to be thought through. This would allow RDAs to concentrate on increasing the demand for skills from employers, recognising that that demand is derived from the need to meet the wider business objectives of firms. This in itself would be a difficult agenda; diverting RDAs off to try and 'plan' education and training provision for individuals is to put an unrealistic burden upon them.

The issue of pay

One key piece of evidence for suggesting that individuals on average make wise choices in relation to learning is that those choices seem to reflect well differences in wage premiums attached to different qualifications. One key piece of evidence that suggests that the UK economy does not face chronic recruitment problems is that pay inflation remains remarkably subdued. This makes the point that one cannot analyse labour markets without looking at the role of pay.

A further issue flagged up by the Chancellor, albeit in the context of the decision over entering the Euro, is that of whether the UK has sufficient local and regional variation in public sector pay to reflect different labour market imbalances. Although national pay setting is the norm in much of the public and indeed a lot of the private sector, in practice there is already much local discretion across sectors in setting pay to reflect local circumstances, with the widespread use of local weighting and so on. As Figure 4.4 shows this results in much higher hourly wages in London and the rest of the South East, once a range of other factors are controlled for, though with only minor variations elsewhere across England and Wales. Moreover, these patterns hold even when we include those occupations dominated by the public sector, though it is clear that regional variations in public sector pay are much lower than for private sector pay. Thus there is already a great deal of regional variation in pay. But is there enough?

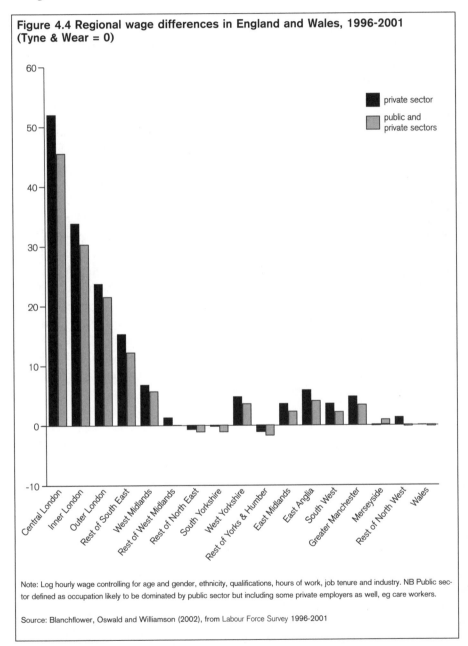

Figure 4.4 Regional wage differences in England and Wales, 1996-2001 (Tyne & Wear = 0)

Note: Log hourly wage controlling for age and gender, ethnicity, qualifications, hours of work, job tenure and industry. NB Public sector defined as occupation likely to be dominated by public sector but including some private employers as well, eg care workers.

Source: Blanchflower, Oswald and Williamson (2002), from Labour Force Survey 1996-2001

If there was too little regional or local variation in pay we might expect a very clear regional pattern to emerge in the incidence of recruitment problems as reported by employers. However, as Figure 3.1 showed, there was little evidence in 2002 of widespread persistent recruitment problems or skills shortages across England: vacancies in England as reported by employers totalled 3.1 per cent of employment, with just under half of these vacancies reported as hard-to-fill and a fifth representing skill shortages. The regional pattern was not glaringly obvious, though with the East, the South East and the South West generally reporting the biggest problems in terms of hard-to-fill vacancies. On the other hand the North West and the West Midlands also had relatively high incidences of skill shortage vacancies. Since this particular survey began in 1999 there has been little in the way of any significant trends, though the incidence of skill shortage vacancies fell sharply in London in 2002. What Figure 3.1 did not reveal is such an obvious 'north-south gap' that would tell us that the labour market was somehow failing in a profound way to allocate labour efficiently in response to recruitment problems across the regions.

This general observation is of course consistent with specific problems such as some public sector organisations having particular difficulties recruiting certain types of labour in certain localities. One question is whether the labour market generally and the public sector specifically is able to respond adequately to recruitment problems when they emerge? A second question is who should bear the higher costs of recruitment to public services in successful congested areas? The paper from which Figure 4.4 is drawn was commissioned by local authorities in the Greater South East to help demonstrate how much more costly it was to recruit staff and to make the case for an enhanced area cost adjustment to the funds made available by central government to help public agencies recruit people in order to provide services. This critical issue is discussed further in Chapter 7.

5. Science, innovation and the regions

The support of innovation would be a key part of any government's national and regional economic policies but debates in this area have the same tendency as others to produce more 'heat than light'. As in many policy areas the Government has been highly active and has brought forward an impressive number of initiatives, but there still remains a sense that there is no strong central narrative in this field (HMT/DTI/DfES 2002). Instead, policy seems to have been driven by vague concepts such as the creation of a 'knowledge-based economy' and by a small number of individuals who have become skilled at promoting their own ideas.

Professor Michael Porter of Harvard Business School, who developed – but more importantly *promoted* – cluster theory, is only the most famous example of such a 'guru-led' approach. Other examples are Professor Richard Florida of Carnegie Mellon University in Pittsburgh who brought us the 'creative class' and the 'Boho Index'; and the Work Foundation who are promoting the concept of the 'Ideopolis'. Without a strong direction in innovation policy policy-makers will adopt too many of these ideas before they are rigorously analysed. It is imperative that an 'evidence-based' approach to innovation policy replaces the 'guru-led' approach we have at present.

The evaluation of innovation

One of the reasons for the lack of an evidence-based approach to innovation policy is the paucity of good evidence from rigorous evaluation. Most genuinely new technologies and cutting edge production processes are produced in relatively few countries by a few world-leaders in companies and research institutions. These are then disseminated and adopted by other firms and across other countries and regions (Griliches 1996). This would suggest that a large element of innovation policy must be a focus on dissemination and on what must seem rather mundane initiatives, such as advances in human resource management or modest improvements in management practice. Evaluation of the true outcome measures of this type of activity is inherently difficult.

Economists would prefer a strict definition of innovation that is susceptible to growth accounting analysis, and are unhappy that we cannot be precise about the contribution of innovation to Total Factor Productivity (TFP). Geographers and regional policy researchers also find that innovation policy does not lend itself to the evaluative mechanisms that they are most used to dealing with, where the focus is on 'jobs created' or 'jobs safeguarded'.

Even given these difficulties, there is an appalling paucity of publicly available evidence evaluating the effectiveness of schemes and what exists is often of limited value. Self-selecting surveys, 'cherry-picking' companies and isolating heroic individuals does not provide robust evaluation. The DTI's Innovation Review (due in the latter half of 2003) needs to take a tough line on the evaluation of programmes designed to support innovation, but it also needs to understand the unique nature of innovation policy. At the very least it should start to develop a methodology by which outcomes can sensibly be measured. As Brooks and Robinson (2003) have argued, the evaluation of innovation is a young science.

How the regions compare

We have argued that innovation should be regarded as a broad concept, which makes it even more difficult to measure differences between the 12 UK regions. The most common proxy used is expenditure on Research and Development (R&D), but this cannot capture all innovative activity. R&D spending is heavily concentrated in manufacturing, and particular parts of manufacturing such as aerospace and pharmaceuticals. This is a key reason why London, for example, has relatively low levels of R&D spending, but this measure almost certainly fails to capture the kind of innovative activity taking place in the traded services sector in London.

There are now attempts to measure outputs, by means of patents and trademarks. However, this is problematic at the regional level. If a car plant in the West Midlands develops a product it wishes to patent, this may be done by the headquarters of an international company in, for example, Germany; by the UK headquarters of this international firm in London; or by the British consortium in the West Midlands that recently purchased the plant. The choice of office to register the patent may have little connection to the region in which the innovative activity is taking place.

The DTI have also recently tried to develop a broader measure of innovative activity by means of a postal survey. Similar surveys are being conducted in all EU countries and the EU Commission has a co-ordinating role. We shall use this survey and the R&D figures to explore regional innovative activity.

Business dominates R&D expenditure: 67 per cent of the total in the UK in 2000. Of the remaining 33 per cent which is public expenditure, 21 per cent is by higher education institutions and 12 per cent by government itself. The regional breakdown for these figures is contained in Figure 5.1. There are clear regional differences in expenditure in each of these three sectors, for example total expenditure in the North East per head was only 18 per cent of that in the East of England. It is within Government spending that the sharpest divides are found: £1 per head in the North East and £78 per head in the South East.

There is, therefore, a fairly clear 'north-south divide' in patterns of expenditure on R&D. Expenditure on R&D is a clearly not a perfect proxy for innovative activity: it is not even a useful measure of innovation inputs. The UK Innovation Survey tries to measure outputs and comes to a very different conclusion. This survey was funded by

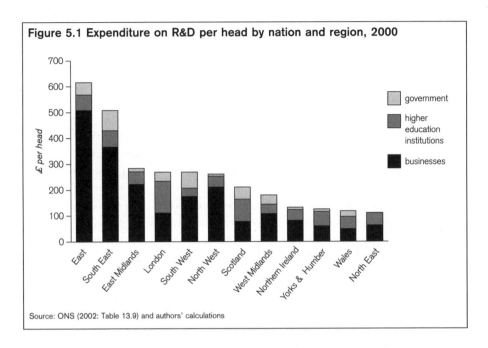

Figure 5.1 Expenditure on R&D per head by nation and region, 2000

Source: ONS (2002: Table 13.9) and authors' calculations

the DTI, conducted by the ONS and is part of the Community Innovation Survey covering the EU. The data is contained in Table 5.1, and the conclusion that the DTI came to was that there were 'few substantial differences between regions on this broad

Table 5.1 Proportion of firms reporting innovative activity, by region

| | Percentage of all enterprises | | | 90% confidence interval |
| | Size of enterprises | | | |
	SME	Large	All	All
East Midlands	47	66	47	+/-5
Eastern	44	71	45	+/-4
London	44	49	44	+/-4
North East	49	89	51	+/-6
North West	43	62	44	+/-4
South East	50	67	51	+/-4
South West	45	68	46	+/-5
West Midlands	51	78	52	+/-4
Yorks & Humber	42	70	43	+/-4
Northern Ireland	45	76	46	+/-9
Wales	45	82	47	+/-5
Scotland	42	73	44	+/-3
UK	46	67	47	+/-1

Source: DTI (2002a)

measure of innovation' (DTI 2002a). This is obviously a different conclusion to that arrived at via examining R&D expenditure, but it is also contrary to perceived wisdom.

Postal surveys do not provide the strongest methodology. It is possible that the survey was unable to control for subjective opinion in its attempts to objectively measure innovation. It is possible that firms in the 'North' have lower expectations than firms in the 'South' and regard certain activities as innovative when their southern counterparts would not and that this affected the survey responses. However, the UK Innovation Survey cannot be simply dismissed as too counter-intuitive without further research.

It may be impossible to come to a firm conclusion on this issue as both sets of data are too flawed to allow us to draw solid conclusions. Some may feel that it is 'obvious' that levels of innovation in the 'North' are lower than in the 'South', simply inferring this from regional differentials in output, employment and productivity. However, it may not be that firms in the 'North' are less innovative, but that there are simply less of them. (Enterprise policy is discussed in Chapter 6). In any case, whether or not there are regional disparities in innovation, the prosperity gap between 'North' and 'South' demands that central government target lagging regions in *all* the seven drivers of regional prosperity, including innovation.

Public policy implications

In this chapter we do not propose to discuss all innovation initiatives of the Government. Rather, we shall focus on three key areas: science policy, the R&D tax credit; and regional innovation policy (including regional innovation strategies, cluster policy, University-Business links and so on).

1   The science base

Science policy is not innovation policy. There is a very strong argument that the Government ought to fund science to expand the sum of human knowledge rather than to improve the productivity of firms. The theory is that, over time, any public money spent on basic research would contribute to the well-being and prosperity of the nation – and that one should not worry too much about exactly what benefits might take place or when they occur.

The Government does not wholly adopt this approach. It demands a more direct relationship between economic or social benefits and funding for science – perhaps because of the increased resources they have been allocated, most recently in the 2002 Spending Review (HMT 2002b). However, government can never be in a position to second-guess which research will be important once completed, and the current

Government does not seem to appreciate the importance of 'research for research's sake'. The £350 million the Government allocates to the Medical Research Council must be for 'maintaining and improving human health' (MRC 2003), not for helping pharmaceutical companies develop profitable products. Similar considerations apply to all seven UK Research Councils (Brooks and Robinson 2003).

Having said that, science provides much of the raw material for innovation. Innovators and entrepreneurs can use the ideas generated by basic research and apply them to 'real world' problems, and physical proximity does seem to enable such exploitation. For example, the growth of electronic clusters in the Thames Valley and Cambridge was closely linked with government science policy (Charles and Benneworth 2000). Putting in place mechanisms that can apply and exploit research is not the same as trying to direct research.

Central Government spends approximately £1 per head on R&D in the North East, while it spends £78 per head in the South East and £62 per head in the South West. Whatever the connection between R&D and regional innovation, it is clear that the large disparities in government R&D spending which currently exist in the UK are inequitable and the science base in all the English regions should be strengthened. The question then arises as to how this can be achieved.

It is worth noting that some RDAs have decided to invest in basic science infrastructure from their own budgets. This has not been in traditional academic and disciplinary forms of research but rather in newer forms of knowledge production typified by collaborative forms of research, and often involving academia, business and NGOs. The industries and areas of research that the RDAs have focused upon are generally conducted via more collaborative methods of research, for example in biotech, nanotech and digitial technologies. This is what Gibbons *et al* (1994) dubbed mode 2 research (mode 1 research being traditional academic research).

One example of this strategy is the decision by the North West Development Agency to contribute £35 million to the merger between UMIST and the University of Manchester (NWDA 2003). Another example is the *Strategy for Success* initiative of One NorthEast and in particular the creation of five Centres of Excellence in the region. This initiative covers both basic science and innovation. One NorthEast itself is spending £200 million over the five financial years 2003-04 to 2008-9, but it is expected that investment from the private sector and EU Structural Funds will increase the overall budget to £500 million. The northern RDAs have presumably felt that funding the basic science infrastructure was an important part of their innovation strategy. As we argued above the link between basic science and 'spin-offs' is not straightforward, and the strategy is inherently risky (particularly the large investment in the North East). However, considering the scale of the challenge facing these regions the last thing we need is timidity.

Notwithstanding these initiatives, the key question over the medium term is whether the science base should be 'regionalised', that is, government spending on science should be spread more evenly across the UK. A recent decision from central government is in fact likely to further centralize the science base. *The Future of Higher Education*, the Government's recent White Paper, committed the Government to the creation of a '6*' rating in the Research Assessment Exercise (the research funding mechanism administered by the four UK Higher Education Funding Councils) (DfES 2003b). The Government's aim was to concentrate resources on the country's 'leading' universities in an explicit attempt to enhance the UK's international position. The universities the Government has in mind are disproportionately located in London and the South East. The research element of the Government's Higher Education policy will work against its regional economic policy.

These are hard decisions to make: do you fund research in the Greater South East and risk exacerbating regional economic disparities; or do you regionalise the science base and potentially harm the overall international standing of UK science? Unfortunately there will not always be a 'win-win' situation. The Government may need to choose between equity and excellence and between the international standing of academia in the UK, and a strong regional policy and full employment. We do not underestimate the difficulty of this decision, but we would urge a centre-left government to give greater priority to regional policy issues. The question then arises as to how the science base could be regionalised, if the Government should decide to pursue that policy.

We suggest that the Government should start identifying key public sector research institutions currently located in the Greater South East which could be moved, over time, to lagging regions. Such a relocation would in itself provide scope for significant job creation, and over time could help improve levels of innovative activity within the region. However, it is the long-term impact that could be most significant. If key decision-makers are no longer sited in the Greater South East there may well be a culture change that will start to address the southern-centric bias in the distribution of UK science spending. (The distribution of public sector jobs is discussed further in Chapter 7).

Within the DTI, the Office of Science and Technology (OST) takes the lead on science, engineering and technology matters. It is based within the London headquarters of the DTI, and employs 150 staff (OST spokesperson 2003). There are seven Research Councils, employing over 6,500 staff in Swindon and nearly 4,000 staff in London and the Council for the Central Laboratory of Research Councils employs 1,800 staff in Didcot (Cabinet Office 2003c). This issue is discussed further in Chapter 7. Relocating these bodies to places such as Merseyside or Teesside would help improve the demand for graduates in these areas, and would send an important signal which would do much to affect the regional bias in science spending indicated above.

A second option is to 'top-slice' new investment in science. This would mean that future investment in science by central government would be divided into two budget headings. The first heading, which would consist of a large majority of the funding, would be open to institutions across the UK. It would follow the same distribution mechanisms that currently exist: rewarding scientific excellence through the Research Councils and the Higher Education Funding Councils. However, a second budget heading might be allocated to regional science with institutions in the Greater South East ineligible for funding under this heading. Such an initiative may help boost science activity in lagging regions.

2   The R&D tax credit

In recent years there has been an international trend away from direct grants and towards favourable tax treatment of R&D expenditure. Tax credits attempt to stimulate business expenditure in R&D by reducing its cost: but also, importantly, by letting firms keep control over the nature and direction of research. With the introduction of the R&D tax credit for small and medium-sized enterprises in April 2000 and for larger firms in April 2002, the UK has now joined several other OECD countries in supporting private sector R&D by this method (Chote, Emmerson and Simpson 2003).

The 2003 Budget estimated that the total cost of the tax credits in 2002-03 would be £600 million (HMT 2003a: Table A3.1). While this is far less than the £1.5 billion of direct government R&D funding for the private sector in 2001, only £190 million of this was for non-defence purposes. The tax credits constitute a significant amount of 'lost' revenue to the Exchequer.

While tax credits apply evenly across the UK, they do have unintended regional consequences. It is the firms which already invest in R&D which are the most likely to take advantage of the tax credits, and it is the firms which invest the most which will be able to make the greatest deductions from their tax bill. As Figure 5.1 demonstrated, these firms are disproportionately concentrated in the South East and in the East of England. If anything, the R&D tax credit is likely to reinforce the uneven pattern of R&D expenditure within the UK. This is not an argument against the R&D tax credit, which will hopefully prove to be a useful policy initiative. It does, however, mean that the regional dimension in other areas of innovation policy needs to be strengthened.

3   Regional innovation

Science policy and the R&D tax credit are 'top-down' policies. They do have regional consequences, but in essence they are UK-wide policies decided by 'the centre'. There are, however, a number of initiatives in innovation policy that are 'bottom-up': regional innovation strategies, cluster policy, business-university collaboration, regional foresight and so on. Responsibility for these instruments lies with devolved and regional institutions, and there are therefore significant variations in policy between the different nations and regions of the UK.

Regional Innovation Strategies (RIS) developed out of the European Union's RIS initiative. In part a mechanism to bring together the key players of the region to design the strategy and to network and spread best practice, it is also designed to try to re-focus existing funding streams on innovation-related activities, for example RSA or EU Structural Funds. RISs are seen as particularly influential in lagging regions as they have proved to be a catalyst for regions that traditionally have had weak networks of innovation (Michie and Oughton 2001).

Traditionally, lagging regions have not easily absorbed funds for innovation (even public funds), leaving prosperous regions to absorb a disproportionately large amount of the funding. This is what has been called 'the regional innovation paradox' (Oughton, Landabaso and Morgan 2001). Improving the innovative capacity of the regions would help to resolve this situation, and in recent years the creation of RDAs in England and the development of RISs across the UK are said to have led to significant improvements in capacity. They are bringing together the three sectors that conduct R&D (business, government and universities) to think broadly about innovation and the local economy. While it is almost impossible to evaluate the contribution of RISs to capacity, or even 'social capital', the fact that they are relatively inexpensive counts in their favour. In England some regions have mainstreamed RISs into the Regional Economic Strategy.

Cluster policy is perhaps the single initiative in innovation policy that has the highest profile. Developed and promoted by Professor Michael Porter of Harvard Business School clusters have become a world-wide fashion, seized upon by policy-makers. They have been defined as:

> Geographic concentrations of interconnected companies, specialised suppliers, service providers, firms in related industries, and associated institutions (for example, universities, standards agencies, and trade associations) in particular fields that compete but also co-operate (Porter 1998: 197).

However, like all fashions cluster policy is now at risk of becoming unfashionable (Martin and Sunley 2002) and numerous criticisms are being made. First of these must be that there has been very little evaluative research: we simply do not know how effective they are as a policy instrument. The DTI must take a more strenuous approach to evaluation in general, and evaluation of clusters in particular. The DTI must rebalance the current policy of 'asymmetric evaluation', where some policy tools (Regional Selective Assistance) are subjected to more rigourous evaluation than other policy tools (clusters).

Another criticism often made of clusters is that the geographical definition varies, and can range from an area where businesses are located closely together, to a network where businesses are much more widespread (an aerospace cluster, for example, could be spread across numerous countries). However, this criticism is far from fatal: it is unrealistic to demand that different businesses work to the same geographies. Business must act as it thinks fit and the state must choose a level at which to conduct public policy. This will almost never perfectly map 'real-world' experience. The regional level seems a more sensible spatial scale to consider clusters than the alternatives of Whitehall or local government.

A criticism often made of clusters, particularly in relation to the English regions, is that there are far too many clusters being supported. This is almost certainly a valid criticism, and the sooner 'market forces' are allowed to operate and thin out the number of clusters the better. However, it is better that some RDAs make mistakes than they have no power or autonomy to innovate.

The most damning criticism of cluster policy is made least of all. It arises from an appreciation that cluster policy should not be regarded as part of regional policy, but is rather a regionally administered form of industrial policy. Policy-makers seem obliged to choose which of the clusters to support (an approach reminiscent of 'picking winners'). This Labour Government has lived in terror of such an idea at the national scale, because of the reputation of previous Labour Governments for subsidising lame ducks. This seems to be the most serious criticism of cluster policy. Even if whole sectors rather than individual firms are chosen, there seems little apparent difference between an approach of 'pump priming' or 'supporting emerging industries' to that of 'picking winners' (Corry 2001). A policy of caution in cluster policy at the national level might be wise.

Another major plank of the Government's innovation policy has been to try to improve the links between higher education and business, and this issue is now the subject of a major review being conducted out of the Treasury by Richard Lambert and expected to report in the Autumn of 2003. It is a subject that has been extensively researched in the past and the conclusions of the Lambert Review will be awaited with interest.

The major difficulty in enhancing Higher Education and business links is the difference in culture between the two arenas. It is unrealistic to expect firms to know in detail how universities work, what expertise exists in local institutions or how the science base may help them in the future. It is also unrealistic to expect universities to understand how the market works, and how much value it would put on the application of their research. Knowledge transfer is sometimes called the third stream of higher education activity, and it is a poor third behind research and teaching. This situation is the natural consequence of differing objectives: industry wants to make profits; Universities want to teach or conduct research that will improve the sum of human understanding. This tension may be less pronounced in non-traditional institutions and in institutes of Further Education but it does still exist. Clearly relationships need to be built up over time and initiatives such as Regional Innovation Strategies, regional science councils and informal networking opportunities will help with this process.

In England, the regional tier is being seen as increasingly important to improving links between universities and businesses (DfES 2003b). Both higher education institutions and business have difficulty in managing relationships with RDAs, but it seems right that RDAs have an important role in this policy area. Furthermore, from 2004-05 RDAs will have a larger role in how the Higher Education Innovation Fund (HEIF) is distributed. The HEIF and funds from RDAs have led to the creation of a number of institutions designed to overcome cultural barriers and try to improve knowledge exploitation within the English regions. These differ from region to region: NorthSTAR in the North East is responsible, via the Science and Industry Council, to One NorthEast; the 15 Centres of Industrial Collaboration in Yorkshire and the Humber report directly to Yorkshire Forward; and KnowledgeNorthWest is a joint initiative between the North West Development Agency and the North West Universities Association.

Conclusion

It is clear that central government needs to promote higher levels of R&D expenditure in the lagging regions of the UK, and the most straightforward way in which this can be done is through its own spending on R&D. There are two methods in which steps can be made in this direction: by relocating institutions to regions such as the North East and Yorkshire and the Humber, where current levels of R&D spending are disproportionately low; and through explicitly creating a regional science fund, possibly ten per cent of the total funding.

Science policy is not innovation policy, and there is no conclusive evidence that firms in the 'North' are less innovative than firms in the 'South'. Nevertheless, innovation is clearly one of the key drivers of prosperity and the Government is right to identify higher levels of innovation as a policy objective. However, we need a more robust approach in this area and the Government should be wary of high-profile academics and consultancies marketing easy answers.

6. Enterprise policy

Enterprise is clearly one of the drivers of both productivity and employment growth in the economy. In *Productivity 3* the Treasury and the DTI stressed that growth of new firms is often associated with the introduction of new technologies, innovative ways of working and increased competitive pressure on other firms. It is through this 'churn' effect that new firms and plants entering the market account for such a significant part of total productivity growth (HMT/DTI 2001). This analysis preceded a discussion of enterprise policy with reference to start-ups only.

Such an analysis restricts debate to entrepreneurs starting new ventures and to small businesses. However, individuals within established firms can generate new ideas or established firms can enter new markets (a recent example is the move by supermarkets to offer financial services to their customers). Unfortunately, the only DTI PSA target that refers to enterprise policy specifically refers to small firms only:

> Help to build an enterprise society in which small firms of all kinds thrive and achieve their potential, with (i) an increase in the number of people considering going into business, (ii) an improvement in the overall productivity of small firms, and (iii) more enterprise in disadvantaged communities (HMT 2002b).

In truth enterprise policy needs to be as relevant to large businesses as small and medium sized enterprises (SMEs), and needs to include all measures designed to improve the capacity of managers and employees to create value out of their available resources (Brooks and Robinson 2003). The government agency that leads on policy on the promotion of enterprise is the Small Business Service, a focus which hinders the discussion of enterprise in *all* UK firms. If the Small Business Service were renamed the Business Service it could serve firms of all sizes as well as help SMEs to become larger firms. Policy debates could therefore be refocused with little institutional upheaval.

What is urgently needed is a more robust debate on enterprise and small firms policy. It is still commonplace to hear that a disproportionate number of new jobs come from small firms, or that a big SME sector is a necessity for a successful economy. It is true that in the 1980s the share of total private sector employment in the SME sector rose substantially, but this trend did not continue during the 1990s. Total employment in SMEs changed little between 1994-1996 and 1999-2001, increasing by less than 2 per cent (TUC 2003). In contrast, almost all the increase in total private sector employment was in large firms, with an increase of 17 per cent. The size of the small firm sector means that it necessarily creates many new jobs, but it is also a sector where large-scale job destruction also takes place. As the TUC concluded:

The conventional assumption that more enterprises must always mean more jobs and fewer enterprises must always.mean less jobs is simply not true under current market conditions (TUC 2003).

A significantly under-utilised source of data comes from the Small Business Service (SBS) at the DTI. Table 6.1 confirms that SMEs have employed a *declining* share of the workforce over the last decade, with data for the period 1997-2001 reported. The SBS data has also allowed for a regional breakdown since 1997. A much higher proportion of the workforce is employed in SMEs in Northern Ireland and Wales. It is noticeable that larger firms employing over 250 people dominate employment in London. There seems little correlation between the proportion of employment in SMEs and regional prosperity – although if anything it may be negative. This is a further reason for questioning why SMEs receive so much attention from public policy.

Table 6.1 Employment by size of business in the UK's regions, 2001

	% of total employment by size of business (number of employees)			
	None	*1-49*	*50-249*	*250+*
UK (1997)	13.6	31.1	12.1	43.4
UK (2001)	12.8	30.6	12.0	44.6
Northern Ireland	15.1	47.5	17.2	20.1
Wales	16.8	38.0	12.4	32.9
South West	16.3	37.0	11.5	35.2
North West	12.0	33.5	13.9	40.6
South East	15.0	31.4	11.9	41.6
Scotland	11.5	32.8	13.6	42.1
East Midlands	11.3	32.1	13.4	43.2
East	13.7	30.7	11.2	44.4
Yorks and Humber	10.9	30.6	12.8	45.7
West Midlands	10.6	30.8	12.7	45.8
North East	10.3	30.4	13.2	46.0
London	11.8	21.8	9.4	57.0

Source: SBS (2003)

Enterprise policy, therefore, ought to try to promote enterprise in firms of all sizes in pursuit of three broader objectives: more net jobs (not more people starting firms); higher levels of productivity; and social objectives (particularly in deprived communities). This chapter will make some generic points about enterprise policy, before going on to discuss the role of enterprise in job creation.

Enterprise policy

Public sector support for small businesses is surprisingly large in financial terms. The Cross Cutting Review of Government Services for Small Businesses (SBS/HMT 2002) estimated total expenditure by public sector institutions in the UK – at the local, regional and national levels – at around £8 billion in 2001-02 (see Table 6.2). The Department of Environment, Food and Rural Affairs contributed just over £3 billion of this financial support, essentially subsidies for farmers. However, this report will not specifically address agricultural support issues. A further £2.6 billion was in the form of revenue foregone through various tax measures. This left £2.2 billion for all the other initiatives. The question arises as to how such diverse schemes, administered by different organisations, can be co-ordinated to achieve a 'joined-up' approach to supporting small businesses, let alone a broader enterprise policy.

The Government has contributed to the complexity of this situation, bringing forward a number of initiatives additional to those it inherited. It has created the Small Business Service, Enterprise Areas, the Business Incubation Fund, the Phoenix Fund, nine Regional Venture Capital Funds, the Bridges Community Development Venture Fund, the University for Industry and the Enterprise Management Incentive. It has also reduced Corporation Tax, created the Community Investment Tax Credit and Business Planning Zones. It has also increased the emphasis on enterprise in schools, and it is now policy that every child should have experience of enterprise by the time they leave school. This is not a definitive list, but it does illustrate the complexity of the Government's enterprise policy.

Improving the standards of external business advice is an important goal of enterprise policy, with imperfect information regarded as a market failure that poses significant obstacles to firms. As small firms generally do not have the resources to employ individual specialists this is one area where a focus on SMEs is justified. One recurring criticism has been that the number of bodies operating in this field is too numerous. Even central government itself now appreciates that the complex situation is a real impediment to getting companies to seek advice.

In 2002 the Better Regulation Task Force examined the delivery of economic development at the local level (Better Regulation Task Force 2002). Taking evidence from a variety of stakeholders the Task Force concluded that a rationalisation of the number of bodies operating on the ground was desirable. Its main conclusion was that RDAs should have responsibility for Business Links Operators (the DTI sponsored delivery arm of the Small Business Service). As discussed in Chapter 4, one of the initiatives contained in the 2002 Spending Review was a pilot initiative to experiment with RDA-led co-ordination and management of Business Links in four regions: the North West, North East, East Midlands and West Midlands. These pilots only became operational from April 2003 so it is too early to judge their success. If successful,

Table 6.2 Government services for small businesses, 2001-2002

body	programmes	estimated cost £m
Small Business Service	UK online, Business Links, Phoenix Fund, STEP, etc	349.0
DTI	Over 100 schemes	160.0
DTI Agencies	Office of Science and Technology, Design Council, Companies House, etc	115.0
British Trade International	Trade Fairs, etc	43.6
DTLR and Agencies	Neighbourhood Renewal, Coalfield Regeneration, etc	107.1
DCMS and Agencies	NESTA, Film Council, Arts Council, Tourist Boards, etc	332.0
DfES and Agencies	Workforce Development, IiP, Small Firm Trading Loans, etc	138.0
DWP	New Deal schemes, Prince's Trust, etc	71.0
Customs and Excise	Business Advice Schemes, etc	31.0
Inland Revenue	Business Support Teams, etc	50.0
RDAs	Variety of initiatives	274.0
Local Authorities	Variety of initiatives	300.0
European Commission	ERDF, ESF	227.0
European Investment Bank	Global Loans, Venture Capital Funding, etc	19.0
DEFRA and Agencies	Over 120 schemes	3,120.0
Tax Measures	R&D tax credit, 10p starting rate for corporation tax, 20p Small Companies corporation tax rate, etc	2,590.0
Total		**7,932.0**

Source: SBS/HMT (2002)

however, the case for Business Links becoming the responsibility of RDAs would be very strong indeed, though there is a prior question to ask about the effectiveness of Business Links.

A great deal of research has tried to establish the characteristics of the more typical successful entrepreneur. One conclusion is that age is an important determinant of entrepreneurship. The Prince's Trust Business Programme is specifically targeted at helping 18-30 year olds start a business. It is co-funded by the Department of Work and Pensions and focuses on those who are unemployed, under-skilled, within or leaving the criminal justice system or leaving care. An evaluation of the scheme conducted for DWP came to some interesting conclusions (Meager *et al* 2003). Over a third of clients were educated to degree level or higher, nearly half had a family background of self-employment, and the clients were disproportionately drawn from the older end of the age range. Furthermore, businesses were more likely to survive if the founders were, *inter alia*, white, older, with a family background of self-employment, educated to degree level and possessing a neutral or adverse attitude to risk-taking (despite the common perception of entrepreneurial behaviour being associated with a propensity to take risks).

This research merely confirms what we have known for some time. The easiest way to promote new enterprises is to focus attention on individuals in their 30s or 40s who are well educated and who have many years' experience of working in a particular sector. In this context it is worth noting that the average age of the winners of the New Economics Foundation's *Inner City 100* awards was 45. A focus on 'young people' is not an effective policy. Meager *et al* (2003) concluded that:

> There is no statistical evidence, however, that participation in Prince's Trust-supported self-employment has any significant impact on subsequent employment or earnings chances over time.

In short, it was concluded that the Prince's Trust Business programme has not made any difference. The DWP must now reconsider its support for this programme and this approach ought to be the model for evaluating a great many other enterprise initiatives.

Enterprise and job creation

It is important to emphasise that we need to promote a *net* increase in the total number of jobs in lagging regions. The Enterprise Allowance Scheme of the 1980s was heavily criticised for merely displacing local jobs. Unemployed individuals, with modest skills, often started businesses in sectors such as vehicle repair, window cleaning or hairdressing. Due to the subsidy available, these new companies were able to charge lower prices and successfully displaced existing companies. However, when the subsidy ran out, other entrants were eligible for the subsidy, were able to charge lower prices and displaced these companies. The creation of new firms in circumstances such as this did little to promote enterprise nor to create genuinely new jobs.

A second lesson to be learnt from experience of the Enterprise Allowance Scheme is to provide the right mode of funding. Funding provided 'up-front' in the form of a loan or a grant is more likely to enable the self-employed to overcome capital barriers to entry, with higher survival prospects. In contrast, funding provided in the form of a regular allowance or through allowing the participants to continue to receive benefit are less successful (Meager *et al* 2003).

In this section of the chapter we shall consider the contribution to employment of social enterprise and Enterprise Areas.

1   Social enterprise

Social enterprise has moved up the political and policy agenda in recent years. Within Whitehall the DTI have embraced the agenda, publishing *Social Enterprise: a strategy for success* (DTI 2002b) and creating the Social Enterprise Unit. The rapid rise of the social enterprise agenda has meant that there is still little or no evidence of the impact of government interventions on social enterprises. In fact, we do not even know the extent of the sector in the UK. The lack of available evidence to the contrary has enabled unsubstantiated claims to be made about the value of promoting social enterprise, in particular that it is an important tool of job creation.

It is important to remember that there are a variety of social enterprises: the co-operative movement, not-for-profit organisations which deal in ordinary working markets, and 'bottom-up' enterprises which foster economic inclusion and are rooted in the social inclusion agenda (Social Enterprise Coalition 2003). This typology is useful as it distinguishes between the social and the economic.

The *social* impact of this sector is clear, but the impact upon *enterprise* is less so. Individuals involved in the schemes do learn new skills, and the employability of individuals from excluded groups might be improved. Furthermore, it is easy to understand the contribution which social enterprises can make to community capacity and social capital. And while enterprising individuals will create jobs in the sector, it is not at all clear that government initiatives in this field are useful in improving economic activity or employment in deprived communities. This is not to say that public institutions should not support social enterprise, but that it should be regarded as part of community involvement and neighbourhood renewal strategies. The contribution to regional economic policy objectives is far from proven.

It is interesting to note that the social enterprise sector has embraced RDAs (Social Enterprise Coalition 2003). However, each of the five statutory purposes of RDAs relates to specifically economic objectives (for example raising employment; furthering economic development and regeneration; promoting business efficiency, investment and competitiveness). It is perfectly understandable for RDAs in regions with full employment, and in regions without demand-side employment problems, to promote social enterprise. The rationale for RDAs in lagging regions is harder to understand. It is part of an unfortunate tendency of many RDAs to lose focus on their primary economic objectives, in particular that of improving levels of employment.

2   Enterprise Areas

The creation of Enterprise Areas was announced in the Pre-Budget Report of 2002. Boundaries are identified using the four indices of multiple deprivation in the four nations of the UK, and are drawn at the ward level (postcode level in Scotland). There are 1997 Enterprise Areas in the UK. Levels of business activity are generally lower in more disadvantaged areas, and measures available to firms within the Enterprise Areas include an exemption from stamp duty, a Community Investment Tax credit, the Bridges Community Development Venture Fund, the Phoenix Fund and support for the Inner City 100 awards. As some of the support available to firms within these areas consists of fiscal measures, they apply across the UK and are administered by Whitehall.

The Government hopes that Enterprise Areas will both raise levels of enterprise and economic activity and meet social objectives: 'supporting enterprise in disadvantaged areas is a vital part of the Government's wider neighbourhood renewal objectives' (HMT/ODPM 2003: Appendix A). The focus on the ward level has created a patchwork of Enterprise Areas: for example, there are 208 in the North East and 17 in Newcastle-upon-Tyne.

A focus on the ward level may be sensible for some neighbourhood renewal objectives, but it is not apparent how it will achieve economic objectives. Deprived wards are not likely to have a high proportion of the mature professionals who are likely to make successful entrepreneurs. A focus on the broader Travel-To-Work Areas (TTWA) would be likely to ensure that Enterprise Areas impact on 30-something potential entrepreneurs. It would also mean that individuals in 'hard-to-reach' communities would be both in Enterprise Areas, should they decide to start a business, but crucially they would also be within travelling distance in case entrepreneurs elsewhere in the Enterprise Area create job opportunities. Such a strategy would be consistent with the Treasury's objective of extending travel-to-work distances. The boundaries of Enterprise Areas and those TTWAs eligible for assisted area status should be aligned.

Conclusion

Generally speaking, enterprise does not spring from the ashes like a phoenix. Nor is it obvious that public policy should give high priority towards encouraging more teenagers to set up in business. Rather the typical successful entrepreneur is more likely to be a mature manager or professional, to be found across all the sectors of the economy. The best contribution regional economic policy can make is to ensure a broad sectoral spread of economic activity in each of the regions, from which new enterprises and entrepreneurs may be spun off. Narrowly defined disadvantaged areas have concentrations of people with characteristics least likely to make them successful entrepreneurs and should not be the target for public policy.

The ward is not the best geographical unit at which to target enterprise policy any more than employment policy. A very long run approach would focus on helping people from disadvantaged areas access jobs over a broad area and develop the experience and skills which may allow them to develop a business idea later in their careers. This is more likely to prove a fruitful approach than trying to grow entrepreneurs from scratch.

7. Public spending and investment

Investment in physical capital ought to contribute towards improving regional productivity and help create and protect jobs. At the national level much of the UK's productivity gap with France and Germany is due to differences in physical capital (plants and machinery) (O'Mahony and de Boer 2002). However, as *Productivity 4* acknowledged 'Data at a regional level show that there is not a strong correlation between the best performing regions and those where capital expenditure is the highest' (HMT/ODPM 2003). It seems, therefore, that levels of private sector investment in physical capital do not easily explain the regional economic disparities that exist within the UK. Levels of public sector investment may be more important in explaining regional disparities and certainly will have a role to play in reducing regional economic disparities. This requires us to look at the way that public spending is distributed across the UK.

Fair funding in public expenditure

All advanced industrial economies consciously redistribute resources across regions and localities to achieve more equitable outcomes in terms of public spending. In some countries with federal constitutions the processes that achieve this are very formalised. As befits a country without a codified constitution, the UK's system of fiscal equalisation has evolved over time in response to particular political pressures and requirements. This does not, however, *necessarily* mean that it is any the less effective at achieving a desirable distribution of resources when compared with other countries.

The UK can be thought of as having a public expenditure system characterised by a division between two types of expenditure (Heald and McLeod 2002). First, expenditure on 'national' programmes, such as defence, or on 'uniform' programmes, such as social security. Expenditure of this type may have differential regional impacts, but these are effectively unintended consequences of UK-wide decisions. The second type of expenditure is undertaken on a country basis, with well-defined and separate systems for Scotland, Wales and Northern Ireland. Changes in this type of expenditure are allocated via the much-misunderstood Barnett system, and there are secondary mechanisms that distribute expenditure territorially within each of the four nations of the UK.

Joel Barnett was Chief Secretary to the Treasury in the 1970s when the current mechanisms were developed during the attempts of the then Labour Government to legislate on devolution. On the original formula, changes in public spending in England on services that were devolved to Scottish and Welsh administrations, were to result in changes to the grant for Scotland and Wales in the ratio 85:10:5 (England:

Scotland: Wales). It, therefore, did not aim to control public spending *per se*, but rather *changes* in public spending. The system was designed to be a temporary system that would be replaced by a 'needs-based mechanism' in time. A flawed and unsubstantial needs-based assessment was conducted, but the in-coming Conservative Government did not act upon it and the Barnett system survives to this day.

The latest figures detailing the national and regional breakdown of public spending are contained in Table 7.1, which details reserved as well as devolved expenditure. Figures for the English regions have only been produced on a basis comparable with the UK's nations since 1998-99. There are quite clearly substantial variations across the nations and regions of the UK: Northern Ireland has the highest levels of public expenditure and the South East the lowest. Clearly the current mechanisms are producing some forms of redistribution, as the lagging regions generally receive higher levels of funding then the richer regions. However, if we assume that there should be an inverse relationship between GVA/GDP per head and identifiable expenditure per head then there are three regions that do not match the general trend. Scotland, London and Northern Ireland each seems to receive higher levels of public expenditure than their relative prosperity would indicate (McLean and Macmillan 2003).

Table 7.1 Trends in total identifiable public expenditure in the UK's nations and regions, 1998-1999 to 2001-2002 (UK=100)

	1998-1999	1999-2000	2000-2001	2001-2002
Northern Ireland	134	134	131	127
Scotland	118	119	120	120
Wales	116	114	113	113
London	114	114	110	113
North East	107	110	110	111
North West	103	104	104	104
Yorks and Humber	96	95	100	99
West Midlands	94	94	94	95
South West	89	90	90	89
East Midlands	89	90	90	90
East	86	87	87	85
South East	86	84	84	85

Source: HMT (2003b)

Table 7.1 will be familiar to many journalists who write for Scottish, Welsh and English regional newspapers. When the Treasury publishes the figures in April each year, they are invariably the subject of much comment. It is in the North East of England that these figures receive the highest profile, and *The Journal* newspaper has run a campaign against the Barnett formula and headlines such as 'On wrong side of £1 billion border' are commonplace (The Journal 2002). However, this is not the opinion on the other side of the border. As Jack McConnell concluded before he became First Minister:

> The Barnett Formula cannot answer all the questions asked of it but its general acceptance historically has led to stable public spending settlements over twenty years. There is still to be a better alternative system put forward (McConnell 2000).

David Heald and Alasdair McLeod (2002) also concluded 'Much of the political attention currently paid to the Barnett formula hinges on the contradictory assertions that it is extravagantly generous to the Devolved Administrations, or that it is imposing destructive financial pressures upon them'.

Table 7.1 also demonstrates that the differences in spending between the different nations and regions of the UK has changed little over the period since devolution took place. In *theory*, the Barnett formula ought to produce a convergence in per capita spending: the so-called 'Barnett squeeze'. As the Barnett mechanisms distribute equal per capita increments to each country, smaller percentage spending increases are automatically delivered to those territories with the highest spending levels. The figures in Table 7.1 would indicate as far as Scotland is concerned, the 'Barnett squeeze' is not yet in operation and concerns on this score would seem to be unfounded as yet. Levels of spending in Northern Ireland, however, may be converging towards the UK average. This could be partly explained by lower security costs due to the peace process, expenditure on which falls to the Northern Ireland Office. It may also be partly explained by the 'Barnett squeeze', which applies to expenditure by the Northern Ireland Government Departments. It is believed that the Department of Finance and Personnel has conducted its own analysis of Northern Ireland's 'needs' which estimated that levels of spending at 125 per cent of spending in England would be 'fair'. Relative levels of public spending seem to be fast approaching this level.

Public expenditure is the one issue that could possibly ignite divisive territorial rivalries in the UK (Morgan 2002). The Barnett formula has been subject to much criticism since its inception, and almost every part of the United Kingdom has individuals and organisations arguing that it should be abolished (Ken Livingstone in London, the SNP in Scotland, Plaid Cymru in Wales (for different reasons than the SNP) and the Campaign for the English Regions in the north of England). However, despite this coalition of criticism it is hard to see how reform of the Barnett formula can be achieved in the near future, given the reluctance of the UK Government to open up the debate. Treasury Ministers will understandably be loath to open up a politically divisive issue when the achievable public expenditure savings are likely to limited (Midwinter 1997). In particular, as a Scottish MP the Chancellor of the

Exchequer will be understandably concerned that levels of spending in Scotland are not disadvantaged. The result has been that, even in those nations and regions that would like to see reform, there is a general consensus that the Barnett system will not be reformed for some time. Unfortunately, recent academic literature in this area – on fiscal federalism, on Grants Commissions, *et al* – are unlikely to be called upon by policy makers for some time yet.

However, debates over the Barnett system are not going to disappear and there are still many public expenditure issues outside Barnett which are relevant to current policy debates. It would be therefore fruitful to consider the principles by which we should judge the fairness of any system of fiscal redistribution across the regions and localities of a country like the UK.

Principles of fair funding

The first basic principle is in essence straightforward: any particular area should be able to offer its residents broadly the same level of public services as another area, regardless of the level of economic prosperity and therefore the tax base in that area. So a less prosperous area in the 'North' with a poor tax base should be able to offer broadly similar services to any area in the 'South' where taxes are more buoyant. In fact it is the only bit of 'quasi-Marxism' that seems to survive in public policy, in that in essence it means for each region 'from each according to their means (tax base); to each according to their "needs"'.

It is this last word that complicates matters: how do we identify needs? The complex funding formulae that are used, for example, to distribute resources to the health service or to fund schools across England, have to try and measure the health or schooling 'needs' of many different areas in a way that is both fair and seen to be fair. Needless to say this is more easily said than done. Any formulae may also try to take into account the different 'costs' that localities face in delivering particular services.

What factors need to be taken into account in constructing a 'fair' formula?

1   The overall population base is the obvious starting point and most funding formulae start with a per capita allocation.

2   There are some 'needs' over which in principle there is broad agreement: those relating to differences in levels of poverty or ill-health, for example. As a result an area such as the North East with very high levels of poverty and ill-health should do well out of any 'fair' formula and London's high rate of child poverty should also be reflected in its allocation of spending.

3   There are some forms of 'need', however, that spending formulae find it difficult to encompass. The problems posed, particularly for London's public

services, by high levels of mobility and transience in schools are one example, as the Cabinet Office (2003a) has noted. Another example might be the higher policing costs in the capital as a result of the location of so many important 'targets'.

4   In relation to 'costs', the higher costs of delivering services in rural areas is usually recognised as something that the central Exchequer should compensate for. This could be one reason why, other things equal, Scotland might receive more resources than the average reflecting the need to provide public services such as schools across the Highlands and Islands. Such rural areas tend not to be particularly affluent so that this type of compensation for higher costs is unlikely to conflict with any assessment based on 'needs'. Any formulae that reflects various forms of social need and higher costs in rural areas is likely to redistribute resources to less affluent areas in a way that would act to *reduce* regional disparities.

5   London and the Greater South East face higher costs in delivering public services because of the need to pay enough to recruit and retain employees in the context of a relatively high demand for certain types of labour in an expensive part of the country. The problem, of course, with such an 'area cost adjustment' is that if a region becomes more economically successful and as a result prices and wages are bid up, more resources will flow into that region to reflect the higher costs of recruiting and retaining staff. In turn those extra resources could further bid up wages and prices. In this case any formulae could act to *increase* regional disparities.

6   Finally some elements of higher spending in an area will reflect conscious policy choices. If Scotland chooses to extend free personal care to all elderly people, in contrast to England where the provision of such care is means-tested, this is precisely the kind of policy choice that devolution should make possible. However, it is also equally clear that the costs of such choices should be borne regionally or locally and not by the central Exchequer. Similarly, if Northern Ireland chooses to have denominational schools, the higher costs of this should be borne by taxpayers in the province.

In reality of course, the ability of the devolved administrations or of local authorities in England to exercise significant policy choices is constrained by the very low proportion of revenue raised locally in the UK's highly centralised tax system. An analysis of spending formulae such as the one used to distribute funding for schools in England, where about 70-75 per cent of funding is on a per capita basis and the balance adjusts for various needs and costs (Johnson 2003), would suggest that this balance between local (70-75 per cent) and central (25-30 per cent) funding would still allow for an adequate amount of fiscal redistribution. In practice of course the ratios of centrally and locally raised revenue in English local government are precisely the other way round.

Some ways forward

Needless to say, reforms to national and local taxation that would significantly reverse the proportions of revenue raised would amount to a bit of a revolution in the UK's fiscal constitution. A proposal to end the 'area cost adjustments' that help compensate the Greater South East for the higher labour costs of providing public services would probably lead to real civil disturbance. And yet public policy is already nudging in the direction that would be suggested by an analysis of the principles of fair funding discussed here. The Treasury is enthused by the idea of a 'new localism' (Balls 2003) which includes at least the beginnings of some thinking about how new revenue streams could be made available to local political institutions.

One of the first examples of this particular type of 'new localism' will be the introduction of a 'prudential' system for capital spending in Northern Ireland. This will allow the Northern Ireland Executive to undertake borrowing to help remedy its widely acknowledged deficiencies in infrastructure investment. Any debt incurred has to be serviced from its revenue base (Brown 2002). This means that Northern Ireland Government Departments are effectively left with little choice but to correct the infrastructure backlog though increased local charging, notably by introducing water charges and by substantial increases in local property rates. (It should be remembered that Northern Ireland has a very different system of local government to the rest of the UK.)

As one of the poorest parts of the United Kingdom, Northern Ireland would not seem to be the obvious starting point for increased regional revenue raising. However, the 'new economic settlement' described above was a response to historically low levels of rates and charges. This does indicate, however, that sometimes there is a political will to introduce greater regional and local flexibility into the UK's centralised tax and public expenditure system. In the rest of this chapter we shall examine how successful regions ought to be asked to make a larger contribution towards meeting the increased costs of success. Many of the policies mentioned here will not be targeted specifically at successful regions, but spatially blind policies will often have a differentiated regional impact.

Transport spending represents an interesting starting point. One myth that needs to be dispelled is the irrevocable link between the growth in road traffic and the economy (Grayling forthcoming). As the Government's trunk roads advisory committee concluded, there is no simple link between transport provision and economic development. The relationship between the two is not always intuitively

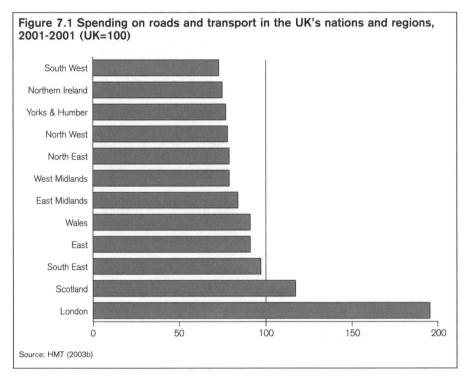

Figure 7.1 Spending on roads and transport in the UK's nations and regions, 2001-2001 (UK=100)

Source: HMT (2003b)

obvious, and there is a complex pattern of effects leading in different directions (SACTRA 1999). It is quite possible to uncouple traffic growth and economic growth. Another myth which ought to be dispelled is the fashion for large-scale 'flagship projects'. Numerous small-scale initiatives, particularly bus services, are likely to be more egalitarian and environmentally sustainable and better value for money than grandiose ribbon-cutting road schemes or extensions to rail or underground services.

The principle that affluent regions with buoyant local tax revenue should bear the costs of extra spending to deal with the problems of congestion is already being put into practice, particularly through the high-profile central London Congestion Charge. Around 80 per cent of Department for Transport expenditure is disbursed in six particular areas (the precise proportions vary year to year): the Highways Agency, the Strategic Rail Authority, the London Underground, the Channel Tunnel, Bus Fuel Grants and central administration (McLean 2003). As the Cabinet Office Strategy Unit pointed out in its analysis of London, transport is one of the few areas of public spending not subject to a spending formula (Cabinet Office 2003a). The Strategy Unit did not point out, however, that the result is that per capita spending on transport in the capital is twice the national average and two-and-a-half times spending in the North East (Figure 7.1). This represents a significant subsidy by the general taxpayer to highly paid professionals using public transport in and around the capital that may be hard to justify.

Similar considerations apply to housing. At first glance, the regional distribution of public expenditure on housing is even more uneven than expenditure on transport, as Figure 7.2 shows. Scotland is the UK region with the highest levels of public expenditure in this policy area, but levels of expenditure on housing within Scotland are determined by the devolved administration under their Assigned Budget. Furthermore, Scottish housing law is very different to that in England and Wales.

London is second to Scotland in terms of expenditure on housing, but the neighbouring East of England region has the lowest levels of public expenditure. Spending per head in London is £197 while in the East of England it is £3. In the South East it is £28 per head.

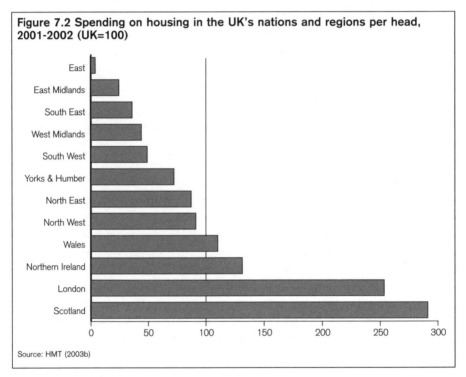

Figure 7.2 Spending on housing in the UK's nations and regions per head, 2001-2002 (UK=100)

Source: HMT (2003b)

Approximately 95 per cent of expenditure on housing in England is made through the Housing Corporation and the Housing Revenue Account Subsidy (McLean 2003). The Housing Corporation registers, funds and supervises registered social landlords in England, and the majority of their expenditure is on capital projects. Over the last few years, there has been a general decline in expenditure in all regions, with the exception of London and the North West. The Housing Revenue Account Subsidy is an ODPM grant scheme which subsidises expenditure by local housing authorities to manage and maintain council property and to encourage authorities to keep rent increases within guideline levels. Expenditure is concentrated in a few regions: North East, North West, London and Yorkshire and the Humber (McLean 2003).

The key issue for policy-makers in housing policy is to manage the very different problems of failing housing markets in the 'North' and shortages of homes in the 'South'. The Government's approach is outlined in *Sustainable Communities* (ODPM 2003a), and deals with these two different problems in different ways. The housing stock in the 'North' is to be modernised and nine housing market renewal pathfinder projects are to be created in the most severely affected areas. In the 'South' there is to be a 'step-change in housing supply' and four growth areas are to be created in London, the South East and the South Midlands (ODPM 2003a). Improving housing supply will be substantially more costly than modernising the housing stock, although the costs of housing market modernisation should not be underestimated. The Government has, therefore, allocated substantially greater sums to the Greater South East than to the 'North'. Table 7.2 is taken from *Sustainable Communities* and shows the higher levels of funding available to the Greater South East, particularly as the Greater South East has only approximately two-fifths of the population of England. Furthermore, the wider infrastructure costs associated with growth are usually substantial: roads will have to be built to new houses, schools and hospitals will have to built for new communities.

Table 7.2 Estimates of resources for the Communities Plan

	02/03	03/04	04/05	05/06	Total 2003/04 to 2005/06
Housing – London, East and South East	995	1,573	1,558	1,605	4,736
Housing – other regions	719	852	892	914	2,658

Source: ODPM 2003a

Some of the above expenditure on housing in the Greater South East is clearly justified. In particular thousands of families with children in London live in Bed & Breakfast accommodation and other unsuitable temporary accommodation, a phenomenon that does not exist to the same degree anywhere else in the UK. This is clearly a need that requires 'fair funding'. However, much of the investment in the Greater South East is not of this type, but is rather the consequence of success. With regard to this latter type of expenditure, the key question again is who should pay?

Section 106 of the Town and Country Planning Act 1990 can be used to enable local authorities to secure the provision of, or improvement to, infrastructure necessary to meet the needs of the occupiers of new development. However, Section 106 powers have not been enthusiastically used by local authorities and the ODPM have indicated that they would like to see a greater share of the land value increase to be captured for local infrastructure. The Government is consulting on Local Authority Business Growth Incentives to allow local authorities to retain a share of the increased business rate revenue associated with growing the business rate tax base locally (HMT/ODPM 2003).

There seems little appetite within Whitehall to develop a replacement for the 'Betterment Levy', the post-war development tax of the Attlee Government. However, there does seem to be the beginning of a more robust approach to trying to capture development contributions and a proportion of the increases in land value arising from growth. Clearly, it is those areas that are growing that will be in a position to raise this revenue: these will be disproportionately but not exclusively located in the 'South'. However, the UK has one of the most centralised tax systems in the developed world and recent moves to create a 'new localism' would seem to imply moves towards greater fiscal flexibility within the UK.

Furthermore, it is the role of central government to balance the territorial dimension of economic and social justice (Adams and Robinson 2002). This task will actually be more straightforward if more of the costs of congestion and development pressures are met locally and/or regionally. Therefore, recent moves towards charging for the costs of congestion and for capturing the value of growth by central government are welcome and should be further developed.

One of the most controversial ways of doing this was unconsciously hinted at in the Cabinet Office Strategy Unit's Analytical Report on London (Cabinet Office 2003a). It pointed out that Londoners have higher incomes and pay more income tax, but the average council tax bill was very similar to the rest of the country. London contributes less in local taxes than it would if the system were more progressive. The inference seems clear: Northern Ireland is not the only part of the UK where local taxes should be increased to fund necessary investment in the public infrastructure or to pay for better public services.

Direct public sector employment

In the 2003 Budget the Chancellor asked Sir Michael Lyons to conduct a review into the scope for relocating public sector activities from London and the South East to other regions of the United Kingdom (HMT 2003a). The Chancellor claimed that successful relocation out of London by private sector companies suggested that the number of jobs relocated could exceed 20,000. The objectives of the review, as stated in the terms of reference, were to explore how relocation might improve both 'the delivery and efficiency of public services; and the regional balance of economic activity.'

Over the years, many jobs and offices have been relocated from London and the South East. For example, the Drivers and Vehicle Licensing Agency (DVLA) was relocated to Swansea in the 1960s and the Patent Office was relocated to Newport in the late 1980s. While the Wilson Government clearly regarded relocation as part of its regional economic policy, it is equally clear that the motivation of the Thatcher Government was to cut costs and save taxpayers' money. The current Government seems equally motivated by the twin aims of cutting costs and benefiting the economies of lagging regions, but also seems to hope that relocation will help improve public services as part of a wider move to modernise the civil service.

Interestingly, the London Development Agency (LDA) has been very supportive of moves to relocate government offices out of London. The nine English RDAs jointly submitted evidence to an inquiry by the ODPM Select Committee (ODPM Select Committee 2003a) into reducing regional economic disparities. This submission stated that:

> In terms of the specific question about whether Government departments, agencies and non-departmental public bodies should be moved to less prosperous regions, we would be in favour of investigating such an approach... It would also help the economy of London and the South East by removing some pressures on housing land as the ability of civil servants to buy houses could increase if departments were located elsewhere (Nine English Regional Development Agencies 2003).

It remains to be seen whether the LDA would support the relocation of senior level jobs, and not just back-office functions. In the late 1980s the then Conservative Government relocated some functions of what is now the Department for International Development to East Kilbride. However, only a minority of Department staff were relocated and the senior management positions remained in London. In contrast to the DVLA and the Patent Office, only secondary functions were relocated from London. As we discussed in Chapter 3, lagging regions generally have a shortage of high-quality graduate jobs though a disproportionate share of graduate jobs in lagging regions are already in the public sector. If one of the objectives of relocation is to help improve the regional economic performance of lagging regions, it would seem imperative to ensure that both senior management and back-office functions are relocated. The relocation of entire Departments and Agencies would appear to be an effective way to achieve this.

The question then arises as to which Departments or Agencies should be relocated out of the Greater South East. If the impact of public sector relocation is to be maximised, the organisations must be chosen with care. The Lyons Review has rightly taken a bold stance in principle and in its guidance to Departments stated that:

The question at the heart of departmental proposals should be: 'why is this function in London/South East?' It might be helpful analytically to start with the presumption that work should not be located in the South, given the enormous extra costs and other disbenefits, with the onus on departments to demonstrate otherwise (Lyons 2003).

We hope that Whitehall will adopt this radical approach and the conclusions of the Lyons Review will be eagerly awaited. In this report we shall not try to match the breadth of the Lyons review, but we will make a few suggestions which might help identify the Departments and Agencies which should be relocated. ODPM has been sometimes styled as the Department for England, as its geographical remit is confined to England and it is responsible for regional and local government policy. Approximately 40 per cent of ODPM staff work already work in the English regions, which means that up 3,500 staff could be relocated (ODPM Spokesperson quoted in *The Journal* 2003).

Figure 7.3 Classification of Whitehall departments

'Mostly English'	'Hybrid'	'Mostly UK'	International Departments
Health	Home Office	HM Treasury	Defence
Education and Skills	Legal Departments	Work and Pensions	Foreign Office
Office of the Deputy Prime Minister	Environment, Food and Rural Affairs	Cabinet Office	International Development
	Culture, Media and Sport	Trade and Industry	
	Transport		

Notes:

A 'mostly English' department has only very modest reserved powers.

A 'hybrid' department exercises functions on behalf of England (or England and Wales) that are carried out on a devolved basis in the territories, with Departments explicitly covering these functions in Cardiff, Edinburgh and Belfast but they also exercise significant reserved powers.

A 'mostly UK' department carries out mostly reserved functions but with some English functions too.

While the ODPM is the most suitable Department to consider for relocation, two other Whitehall Departments are also effectively England-only Departments (see Figure 7.3) and should be considered for relocation. On 1 April 2002 the Department for Education and Skills employed 2,260 civil servants in London and the South East, while the Department of Health employed 2,830 civil servants (Cabinet Office 2003b). It is worth noting that the two largest employers of civil servants in London and the South East are the Ministry of Defence (25,600 on 1 April 2002) and the Department for Work and Pensions (23,050 on 1 April 2002). The response of the DWP to the Lyons Review will be particularly important, in light of the importance of that Department to the regional economic agenda.

In Chapter 5 we argued that the geographical distribution of institutions of scientific research was biased towards the Greater South East, so it would fit with the needs of the English Regions, Wales and Northern Ireland to consider relocating some of the institutions which deal with science policy. The two bodies through which the majority of government support for science spending is channelled are the seven Research Councils and the four Higher Education Funding Councils (one for each of the four nations of the UK). Furthermore, the Office of Science and Technology is based within the London headquarters of the DTI and employs 150 staff (OST Spokesperson 2003). Relocating these bodies would not only be an important employment generating measure, it might over time help to change the cultural attitudes which distribute such a disproportionately large degree of funding to the Greater South East.

Table 7.3 Relocation of Departments and Agencies

	Location	Employment rate (TTWA) %	Staff employed
Medical Research Council	London	71.4	3,945
Biotechnology & Biological Sciences Research Council	Swindon	82.5	3,219
Natural Environment Research Council	Swindon	82.5	2,590
Council for Central Laboratory of Research Councils	Didcot, Oxford	82.9	1,800
Engineering & Physical Sciences Research Council	Swindon	82.5	317
Particle Physics and Astronomy Research Council	Swindon	82.5	302
Higher Education Funding Council for England	Bristol	80.9	223
Office of Science and Technology (DTI)	London	71.4	150
Economic and Social Research Council	Swindon	82.5	111
Design Council	London	71.4	50
Total			**12,707**

Source: Cabinet Office (2003c), OST spokesperson (2003)

The terms of reference of the Lyons Review is to consider relocation from London and the South East, but as Table 7.3 demonstrates a number of these scientific bodies are sited in the M4 corridor in South West England. Places like Bristol and Swindon are areas of full employment with many of the same pressures on development as

London. There is no reason why they should not be considered for relocation under the Lyons Review. As Table 7.3 details, nearly 13,000 staff are employed by these bodies (the three higher education funding bodies outside England are not covered for obvious reasons). It is suggested that these nine bodies are relocated to areas with real labour market weaknesses.

Table 7.3 is meant to serve as an indication of the types of agencies that could be relocated given the discussion on science and innovation in Chapter 5. It is in no way supposed to be an exhaustive list. The outcomes from the Lyons Review are still to be awaited, but the approach adopted – that Whitehall departments must justify why they should stay in the Greater South East – is the correct one.

The issue of where these jobs are relocated to is as important as where they are relocated from. They should not go to relatively prosperous cities such as Leeds, but to cities and towns with low employment rates and a lack of jobs in the higher level occupations. Public sector relocation is one important instrument for helping such places retain graduates.

Conclusion

There is unfortunately little likelihood in the near future of a wholesale revision of the system by which public spending is distributed across the nations, regions and localities of the UK. However, the pattern of public spending is an obvious policy instrument that government can wield to address regional economic disparities. The needs of prosperous regions as well as lagging regions need to be addressed, but in the context of allowing successful regions and localities to raise more revenue to address their needs.

Some Whitehall departments, especially those with an England-only remit, should be relocated to towns and cities with low employment rates, along with key education and science funding bodies. Greater fiscal devolution will at some point need to accompany political devolution, but the starting point for this debate needs to be some agreement on the principles that should underlie a fair funding regime.

8. Governance issues

Increased capacity at the regional level is one of the key principles upon which Labour's new regional policy has been built. Building regional institutions and enhancing the autonomy of those regional institutions is, it is claimed, what distinguishes current regional policies from their predecessors:

> Our new regional policy is based on two principles – it aims to strengthen the essential building blocks of growth – innovation, skills, the development of enterprise – by exploiting the indigenous strengths in each region and city. And it is bottom-up not top-down, with national government enabling powerful regional and local initiatives to work by providing the necessary flexibility and resources (Balls 2000).

This commitment to bottom-up policies is informed by a fairly widespread academic consensus that regional institutional capacity matters to economic performance (Harding *et al* 1996, Russell Barter 2000). The creation of the RDAs and Regional Chambers in Labour's first term were decentralising reforms, which will be welcomed by those who feel that governance in the UK is still too focused on Whitehall. RDAs have clearly become influential players in regional debates, and have worked to improve regional capacity in a variety of ways, particularly through the Regional Economic Strategies, which try to bring together all the relevant stakeholders in the region. The first editions of these strategies have been criticised for being 'wish-lists' and the revised strategies will need to forge a clearer sense of priorities.

However, the role of elected regional governments in achieving economic growth is more contested. One stream of academic opinion is that the link between elected regional government and improved economic performance 'remains unproven and underexplored' (Harding *et al* 1996) and that while democracy may be an intrinsically good thing 'its implications for economic development are more ambiguous than we may care to admit' (Morgan and Rees 2001).

Other academics stress the importance of elected assemblies in delivering policies matched to the diversity of regional conditions, and their role in providing strong political leadership and regional consensus building (Tomaney *et al* 2003). It is argued that if the assemblies help to galvanise their regional economies, mobilising resources which were hitherto untapped and ill-organised for example, then they would have a positive role to play in regional economic renewal. This approach has resonance with the Government and others supportive of regional devolution, for example Peter Mandelson MP:

we cannot achieve economic revitalisation in the North East without modernising the means of delivering our economic policies, and this means renewing the region's political institutions (Mandelson 2001).

So what can we conclude from this discussion? First, it is important to emphasise that strong regional institutions are important for regional economic growth: the Government is right to recognise that regional policy cannot be run from the centre. Second, that regional devolution may be a necessary but not a sufficient precondition for any reduction in regional economic disparities. The case for regional devolution may be stronger on democratic and public service delivery grounds. Third, that the impetus for regional devolution is likely to have come from dissatisfaction with the way that recent UK governments have treated the lagging regions, politically as well as economically. While the impact of devolution and regional assemblies upon economic performance will not be capable of independent assessment for some years, it is quite clear that the record of Whitehall in reducing regional economic disparities is far from distinguished.

The bottom-up emphasis of Labour's new regional policy poses another question: what is the role of Whitehall in this regionalised regional policy? Until recently the Government could be criticised for merely 'passing the buck' to devolved administrations and regional institutions, expecting the simple fact of their creation to start addressing regional economic disparities and refusing to articulate the role of the UK government. However, there is some cause for optimism in this regard.

In the post-devolution world the role of Whitehall in economic governance matters is a complicated one. There is a mix of reserved, devolved and concurrent powers that vary between Scotland, Wales, Northern Ireland and London. There will even be significant variations in policy between the eight RDAs accountable to Whitehall. However, a nation state with devolved and regional polities is still a nation state, and Whitehall and Westminster retain a responsibility for all parts of the UK. Such responsibilities must be exercised in a way that is compatible with the various devolution settlements and must seek to achieve social and economic justice between the various nations and regions of the UK (Adams and Robinson 2002).

As there is no strict and watertight division of competences between reserved and devolved matters, Whitehall and the devolved administrations need to work particularly closely together. The main instrument for inter-governmental relations within the UK are the Joint Ministerial Committees (JMCs), regular summit meetings between Ministers and officials from Whitehall and devolved administrations. Inter-governmental relations within the UK have been surprisingly smooth, but the institutions have not met often. The decision to hold a JMC on the economy towards the end of 2003 is to be welcomed. The Chancellor of the Exchequer will chair the event and it will discuss 'how reserved and devolved policies can best work together to improve economic performance and productivity across the UK' (Scotland Office 2003). This is a welcome recognition that Whitehall has some responsibility for the economies of devolved territories and that the devolved administrations cannot solve regional economic disparities on their own. As we suggested in Chapter 1 it could be the appropriate forum to discuss a new target for narrowing absolute disparities in economic prosperity in the UK as part of the Spending Review 2004 process.

Clearly the concept of territorial justice needs to be fleshed out in the years ahead. Building on the work of ippr's Social Justice Commission (1994), we would submit that a hierarchy of four principles underpin territorial justice. First, that each region and locality should be treated fairly and equitably by the centre. Second, that each region and locality is entitled to be able to meet their needs, whether through raising their own revenue or through transfers from the centre. Third, that territorial justice requires more than just meeting basic needs, and that we need to be concerned with the distribution of opportunity. Finally, that while not all inequalities are unjust; unjust inequalities should be reduced and where possible eliminated. We would also argue that territorial justice should not be defined as a subtractive and inhibiting force, which merely takes things away from successful regions and localities and gives them to the unsuccessful. It has to attend to need, but in doing so it ought to also be an enabling force for all areas and encourage aspirations to improve their economy and the quality of life for inhabitants.

If the UK government is to uphold the principle of territorial justice and make inroads into regional economic disparities, it will need to fundamentally re-address its role in many of the areas highlighted in this report. Examples include employment policy (Chapter 3), science and innovation policy (Chapter 5) and public expenditure and taxation (Chapter 7). Hard decisions will have to be made in the Spending Review 2004 process and while it is encouraging that the Government is asking the right questions, it is not yet clear that it will be bold enough to pursue the right answers.

One of the traditional concerns which academics had with the devolution process was that 'devolution inevitably involves a promotion of bottom-up forms of territorial competition' (Gordon 2002). These concerns do not yet appear to be borne out. Despite the breadth of regional policy instruments, fears over territorial competition mostly focused on two policy areas: inward investment and public expenditure. In the current climate the former may be becoming less important as a tool of economic development, and while there seems no appetite within the Treasury to re-open debates over the fiscal constitution and the Barnett formula (Chapter 7) this debate is likely to gather pace over time. There have been real disagreements between different parts of the UK, for example over the decision by the DTI to move science facilities from Daresbury in the North West to Oxford in the South East. However, this does not amount to a new era of territorial competition and fears on this score do not yet seem justified.

It is worth noting the remarkable levels of access that the RDAs have within central government. Regular meetings are held with the Chancellor of the Exchequer, the Deputy Prime Minister and the Secretary of State for Trade and Industry. Whitehall regularly increases the powers available to the RDAs: more flexibility and the single-pot, powers over tourism and, should the pilots be successful, the possibility of becoming responsible for the Business Links Network. Collectively the RDAs have developed a strategy to influence all Government Departments in Whitehall, and each RDA is allocated specific policy areas to lead upon and specific Whitehall departments to lobby. For example Advantage West Midlands leads on transport issues and relations with the Department for Transport and the South West RDA leads on tourism and culture policy and on relations with the Department for Culture, Media and Sport.

While the RDAs are generally regarded as being successful 'voices for their region', their research capacity has been criticised. The poor quality of available regional data has clearly been a hurdle to the work of the RDAs in trying to analyse regional economies, and unfortunately many have had to commission consultants to produce further evidence of variable and sometimes dubious quality. As a group, the RDAs should collectively fund an England-wide research unit, which could be located in any of the nine regions but which preferably should be located in one of the lagging regions. Others with an interest in this subject might also be involved. The Core Cities Group is a mechanism by which the local authorities of the eight large cities in England come together for common purpose: Newcastle, Leeds, Sheffield, Liverpool, Manchester, Birmingham, Nottingham and Bristol. This group should be interested in improving their empirical research in this field (ODPM *et al* 2003). An England-wide focus on evidence-based policy, the empirical analysis of data and public policy priorities would add much to public debates, leaving individual RDAs and the Core Cities to work on 'foresight' or 'scenario-setting' if they so choose.

Square pegs in round holes?

Since 1999 the UK has been undergoing a period of sustained increases in funding for public services. It is crucial that the instruments of the state – Whitehall, devolved administrations, regional institutions and local government – ensure that public expenditure is used effectively. An important part of this process will be to ensure that policies are designed and administered at the most appropriate spatial scale. If the wrong spatial scale is chosen the result will be poorly delivered services and wasted taxpayers' money.

The problems of ensuring joined-up government have received a great deal of attention recently. Clearly it is sensible for government to strive to ensure that policies interact positively 'on the ground' and that different funding streams, possibly administered by different authorities, complement each other. However, the question that ought to precede debates about joined-up government has received much less attention in policy debates in recent years: at which geographical level should different policies be pursued?

It might be useful to examine one issue in particular to illustrate this problem. It has often been argued that the concentration of economic inactivity in certain parts of large urban centres means that action designed to rectify this situation needs to be focused on these areas (see, for example, Webster 1999). Such an approach might sound attractive at first, but is unlikely to be effective in principle: the geography of misery is different to the geography of recovery.

As we argued in Chapter 3, the most effective spatial scale to analyse labour market issues is the Travel-To-Work Area (TTWA). This has the advantage of being demand-led, the boundaries are drawn following an assessment of a sample of the travel patterns of individuals in the Census. A focus on a more local level betrays a misunderstanding of how the labour market works and reduces the effectiveness of state action. If jobs are created in a local area, there is no reason why better qualified people from outside the area (but within the TTWA) could not successfully apply.

A much more effective strategy would be to analyse the labour market across the whole TTWA and create jobs in those areas attractive to employers. Take, for example, the South Wales mining areas. It would be more difficult to create jobs in relatively inaccessible former mining villages such as Abertridwr or Nelson than in Caerphilly. Good quality transport links (probably buses) would ensure that job opportunities are linked up with areas with high levels of economic inactivity.

As this discussion has demonstrated, the appropriate spatial scale at which to think about labour market interventions is the TTWA, although the interventions themselves could be carried out by regional or local institutions. Decisions relating to planning and major infrastructure investment in areas such as transport and housing would seem to lend themselves to a similar geography. Physical regeneration would seem to be sensibly done at a more local level. Enterprise Areas seem to be at such a small spatial scale that their effectiveness must be questioned. Public involvement and community renewal issues have most resonance at the very local level, even down to particular streets, although the problem then arises as to how you connect this to decision-making at a broader spatial scale. While the problems of joined-up governance must never be ignored, the geography of governance must first be correctly decided.

This is not the only type of spatial debate that needs to be held within the UK. The tensions between national economic policy and regional policy have been the subject of heated debates for many years. This particular debate is complicated by the fact that the distinction between national industrial and regional policy is not straightforward (Gillespie and Benneworth 2002). Industrial policy may be spatially blind, and as such it is quite distinct from regional policy; for example, in privatisation, technology policies, science policies and so on. These policies will generally have different regional impacts, but these are often effectively unintended consequences.

However, industrial policy can also be spatially sensitive and policy-makers might frame them in such a way as to raise the economic performance of lagging regions. In such cases they become synonymous with regional policies, for example policies for the automotive sector could be specifically intended to help the West Midlands economy. To complicate matters further, national industrial policies might be administered at the regional level, but this does not mean they become regional economic policies. An example would include using RDAs to administer, with little regional autonomy, a UK manufacturing strategy.

To this traditional tension between industrial and regional policy must be added a new tension, which arises from the Treasury's productivity agenda. The Treasury have been the driving force behind the renaissance in regional policy in recent years, and their motivation has been explicitly to ensure the regions play their part in improving the UK's productivity record as measured against other nations, particularly France, Germany and the USA. As we argued in Chapter 3, it is not at all clear that this reflects the concerns of lagging regions themselves, indeed in their economic agenda the Welsh Assembly Government have prioritised employment over productivity. Perhaps the Treasury's approach could best be described, to paraphrase former US President Kennedy, as 'ask not what your country can do for your region, but what your region can do for your country'.

Spatial subtlety is also necessary at the sub-regional level. Regeneration initiatives such as the Neighbourhood Renewal Fund and the New Deal for Communities are disproportionately focused on poorer regions and so could contribute towards reducing regional economic disparities. However, regeneration initiatives have a number of objectives, not all of them economic. For example, the stated objectives of the current neighbourhood renewal strategy are the goals of 'lower worklessness and crime, and better health, skill, housing and physical environment' (SEU 2001). Clearly this is an ambitious vision and one which requires numerous different policy interventions before it can become a reality, but not all of these interventions will be most effective if designed and administered at the local level. In particular, an objective to ensure lower worklessness necessitates interventions at the level of the broader Travel-To-Work Area.

In an era of multi-level governance, the fact is that a modern state cannot work on the basis of watertight divisions of functions and competencies (Keating 2002). This is not merely a fact of life that has to be accepted, it is necessary to ensure that the public sector is effective in its interventions. However, it does mean that policy-makers have to be clear about the objectives of policy, clear about which policy tools are most appropriate, clear about at which spatial scale these policy tools should be designed and administered, and clear about how they will interact in practice 'on the ground'.

It is the people who most rely on government action and strong public services that suffer most from such failures of co-ordination.

Regionalising Whitehall

We have argued previously that Whitehall has a quasi-federal responsibility to tackle social and economic inequalities across the nations and regions of the UK (Adams and Robinson 2002). Its inability to understand when it is operating on an English basis, when it is performing UK-wide functions and when it is performing quasi-federal responsibilities militates against this. Furthermore, the failure to appreciate the spatial implications of England-wide or UK-wide decisions means that many Whitehall decisions actually aggravate territorial injustices within the UK.

Before Whitehall departments can 'mainstream' the regional dimension into their spending decisions they first need to identify the amount of expenditure in each region. At present in the English regions, this cannot be done with any certainty. Research suggests that a number of Whitehall departments have made serious mistakes in the information passed to HM Treasury on the regional pattern of departmental expenditure (McLean 2003). This research concluded that in *Education* the published tables understated expenditure in London by £552 million, and overstated it in the East of England by £329 million (discrepancies of around 10 per cent). In *Law, order & protective services* the published tables understated expenditure in London by £443 million (about 12 per cent) and overstated it in the East of England by £110 million (about 7 per cent). And in *Agriculture, forestry, fisheries and food* the published tables overstated expenditure in London by £226 million and understated it in East of England by £254 million (discrepancies of almost 50 per cent). These figures should be seen as an embarrassment for Whitehall.

This research highlighted a number of instances where the actions of central government have not been regionally sensitive. In Chapter 5 we detailed the inequitable distribution of central government science spending, where £1 per head is spent on research and development in the North East while £78 is spent per head in the South East and £62 per head in the South West. In Chapter 7 we discussed the inequitable distribution of spending on roads and transport in the UK. In that chapter we also noted that the 2003 Communities Plan allocates billions of pounds of public expenditure more for the Greater South East than for the 'North' (ODPM 2003a). Many in the 'North' also feel that the Greater South East has a disproportionate share of so-called 'flagship projects': the Dome was sited in London, not Birmingham; the new national sports stadium was sited in London, not Coventry; and London is bidding for the Olympics after the successful Manchester Commonwealth Games.

This report has argued throughout that central government has a very difficult role to play in fulfilling its responsibility of balancing the different, and often competing, interests of the various parts of the UK. However, on balance we would submit that Whitehall does not sufficiently prioritise the needs of lagging regions (although we do recognise the very real needs of London, particularly in the area of child poverty). We back the Government in their commitments on full employment and reducing regional economic disparities but feel that they need to do more if they are to achieve these ambitious goals.

Clearly changing attitudes in Whitehall is not an easy task and will be a long-term process. In the run-up to the 2002 Spending Review the Government did attempt to introduce an element of regionalism into its decision-making processes. They invited the RDAs and the Government Offices to set out their views on the key priorities that would promote prosperity in their regions. The Spending Review revealed that five priorities could be identified from this process: skills and education, transport, broadband, enterprise, and innovation (HMT 2002a). Clearly these are very broad policy areas, to say the least, and cover four out of the Treasury's five productivity drivers (the fifth, competition, having only small spending implications). The devolved administrations are similarly consulted on the Spending Review process, but this process is significantly different as it is not specifically limited to the economic agenda and because the Spending Review process post-devolution has less resonance in Scotland, Wales and Northern Ireland than in England.

It is not clear how this process affected the final decisions made in the 2002 Spending Review, if at all. It may have been a useful exercise in consulting with regional stakeholders and assessing how regional priorities differ within England, but in essence it is a bottom-up process. It is not the same as central government itself juggling the interests of the different territories of the UK. Clearly the Spending Review process is the correct forum in which to decide on issues of territorial justice, as it is where the Government decides on the full range of public policy objectives and associated spending priorities. If issues of territorial justice and quasi-federal responsibility are going to be taken seriously by central government, this is where it matters most.

Conclusion

The setting up of regional economic or political institutions was always unlikely in itself to be a sufficient means for addressing regional economic disparities across the UK. It is taking an inordinate amount of time for Whitehall to understand its role in the post-devolution UK. The 2004 Spending Review represents a unique opportunity for Whitehall to show that it understands the regional agenda. This means firstly, that each Whitehall department will look at the regional impact of its spending patterns. Secondly, Whitehall should invite the devolved administrations to discuss a new PSA target to tackle economic disparities across the nations and regions of the UK. There is no reason why Northern Ireland and Wales especially, but Scotland also, should not welcome such an initiative. Signing up to a common objective is entirely compatible with the operation of different policy instruments in pursuit of that objective as facilitated by devolution. It would show that the DTI and HMT were learning about their quasi-federal functions as UK Departments of State.

9. A modern regional economic policy

The political priority given to regional economic policy is important. There are two broad reasons why closing long-term differentials in regional economic performance matters: improving economic efficiency as unbalanced growth can undermine national economic performance; and there is a straightforward equity dimension, as reducing disparities in prosperity across the UK is important for improving individuals' life chances.

For the centre-left, and for a centre-left government, it is the pursuit of equity that should be the strongest justification for a strong regional economic policy. This does not mean that a situation where the 12 nations and regions of the UK have exactly the same levels of GDP per head is either a realistic or desirable outcome. But while not all inequalities are unjust, unjust inequalities need to be tackled and eliminated. We would submit that the systemic regional economic disparities that have existed in the UK for generations are quite clearly inequitable. The perception that national UK-wide institutions have systematically failed to address this problem exacerbates the sense of injustice and is a cause of dissatisfaction with the UK's political institutions.

It is encouraging that perhaps the most important of those UK-wide institutions is now the strongest of regional 'champions'. While the Deputy Prime Minister has traditionally provided a regional voice, this has been supplemented by the rise of HM Treasury as an advocate for regional policy. The challenge for the Government now is to move beyond its first-term policy of treating unequal territories equally, to a true regional economic policy: one which targets lagging regions in order to narrow absolute gaps in economic prosperity. In this report we have tried to examine how this might be done.

As the Government's new regional policy develops it needs to understand which problems are common amongst UK regions and which problems differ. The needs of London often will be different to those of Northern Ireland, and the needs of North East England will differ to those of South West England. Different problems will need different solutions. This means that regional institutions need freedoms and flexibilities but it also means that central government must appreciate regional circumstances and resist the temptation to become 'spatially blind'.

Furthermore, the Government needs to commit to regional economic policy for the long-term. Regional economic disparities have developed over generations and it will take a significant amount of time to eliminate them. It is important to remember that while the Government needs to set itself a radical objective, it may be that incrementalism is the only route which will achieve the goal of balanced economic growth. Most major change is made up of incremental steps and the 'big bang' approach is the exception not the rule.

While this is a policy area which has been the attention of much academic debate, most of this work has focussed on conceptual thinking and analysing the scale of the problem. Little research has thought through practical policy solutions. However, this is exactly the type of support which policy-makers require. The Government will have drafted its Delivery Plan setting out initial thinking on how the 2002 PSA target of reducing the persistent gap in growth rates between the English regions will be achieved. This was a specific requirement of the original target, which stated that Whitehall Departments would have to 'define measures to improve performance' (HMT 2002a). As negotiations begin on the 2004 Spending Review the onus is upon the Government to show that these measures are likely to actually start addressing regional economic disparities.

Throughout this report we have tried to identify our own practical policy solutions and bring forward our own 'ten-point plan'. The implications of meeting the Government's PSA target are significant, and the implications of meeting the simpler but more radical target we suggest of narrowing absolute disparities in prosperity are even more demanding. We have mapped out below some possible new routes to a regional economic policy that the Government might follow.

Ten point plan for regional economic policy

1 The 2004 Spending Review should set out an unambiguous target to narrow disparities in output per head across the UK nations and regions. The Joint Ministerial Committee on the Economy taking place later in 2003 should be used to agree a target between the Government and devolved administrations.

2 Employment should be given equal weight with productivity as the focus for regional economic policy. Policies are required to increase the demand for labour in the Assisted Areas, which should be re-defined to cover groups of Travel-To-Work Areas in lagging regions with employment rates at or below 70 per cent so that regional policy instruments can be concentrated.

3 The EU should back the UK position of 'renationalising' regional policy. HM Treasury needs to commit significant additional resources to compensate lagging regions for lower levels of EU spending. Regional and local institutions must decide how that funding is allocated across different areas of spending.

4 More good quality jobs need to be created in lagging regions to retain graduates. Increasing the proportion of young people and adults with adequate basic skills and level 2 qualifications are the correct priorities for promoting employment. A period of stability in the administration of learning and skills policy is required.

5 The Government should 'regionalise the science base' by relocating key institutions and by 'top-slicing' new spending on science for lagging regions. The current concentration of government R&D spending and science institutions in the Greater South East is inequitable.

6 The Government needs to rationalise services for small and medium sized enterprises as the number of initiatives and bodies in this area are impossibly complex. In particular, if the current pilots are successful the case for RDAs assuming responsibility for Business Links will be very strong.

7 All Whitehall departments need to 'mainstream' the regional dimension into their spending decisions. Decisions in areas such as housing, transport and science policy need to reduce regional disparities not reinforce them.

8 Prosperous regions and localities should bear more of the costs of extra spending required to deal with the problems of success. Congestion charging and capturing increases in land values can only be the start of something bigger in terms of fiscal reform.

9 Several Departments and Agencies should be relocated from the Greater South East to the lagging regions, such as the ODPM, the Higher Education Funding Council for England and the seven Research Councils. The Lyons Review must relocate senior staff as well as back-room staff.

10 A central research unit for the RDAs and the Core Cities should be created to help promote evidence-based policy-making. This should be located in one of the lagging regions.

References

Adams J and Robinson P (eds) (2002) *Devolution in Practice: public policy differences within the UK* London: ippr/ESRC

Amin A, Massey D and Thrift N (2003) *Decentering the Nation: a radical approach to regional inequality* London: Catalyst

Armstrong H (2003) 'Regional Selective Assistance' *Presentation to ippr Seminar* 7 April

Armstrong H (2001) 'Regional Selective Assistance: is the spend enough and is it targeting the right places?' *Regional Studies 35.3*

Arup Economics and Planning (2000) *Evaluation of Regional Selective Assistance 1991-1995* London: Arup Economics and Planning

Balls E (2003) *Growing the Economy: the local dimension* London: The Smith Institute

Balls E (2000) 'Britain's New Regional Policy: sustainable growth and full employment for Britain's regions' in Balls E and Healey J (eds) *Towards a New Regional Policy: Delivering growth and full employment* London: The Smith Institute

Balls E and Healey J (2002) 'The Regional Economic Challenge' in Engel N (ed) *Age of Regions: meeting the productivity challenge* London: The Smith Institute

Balls E and Healey J (eds) (2000) *Towards a New Regional Policy: delivering growth and full employment* London: The Smith Institute

Barlow Report (1940) *Report of the Royal Commission on the Distribution of Industrial Population* London: HMSO

Belt V, Hentley J, Charles D, Jones I, Audas R and Conway C (2002) *North East Graduate Labour Markets 1999-2000* Newcastle: Centre for Urban and Regional Development Studies

Better Regulation Task Force (2002) *Local Delivery of Central Policy* London: Cabinet Office

Blanchflower D, Oswald A and Williamson B (2002) *Estimated Regional Wages Relativities for England: a report for the South East Area Cost Adjustment Group and Association of London Government* Available at www.nera.com/wwt/publications/4975.pdf

Blitz R and Chung J (2003) 'Back-Slapping and Handshakes Turn to Failure, Criticism and a Commons Grilling' *Financial Times* 23 July

Boldrin, M and Fabio C (2001) 'Inequality and Convergence in Europe's Regions: reconsidering European regional policies' *Economic Policy 32*

Brewer M, Clark T and Goodman A (2002) *The Government's Child Poverty Target: how much progress has been made?* London: Institute for Fiscal Studies

Brooks R and Robinson P (2003) *Manufacturing in the UK* London: ippr

Brown G (2002) 'New Economic Settlement for Northern Ireland: barracks and prisons to be replaced by business and prosperity' *Press Release 42/02* 2 May London: HM Treasury

Burkitt N and Robinson P (2001) 'Overview and Recommendations' in Burkitt N (ed) *A Life's Work: achieving full and fulfilling employment* London: ippr

Cabinet Office (2003a) 'London: analytical report' *The Prime Minister's Strategy Unit* Available at www.pm.gov.uk/output/Page4069.asp

Cabinet Office (2003b) *Civil Service Statistics 2002* Norwich: The Stationery Office

Cabinet Office (2003c) *Public Bodies* Norwich: The Stationery Office

Charles D and Benneworth P (2000) 'Clustering and Economic Complexity – regional clusters of the ICT sector in the UK' Paper presented to *Do Clusters Matter in Innovation Policy?* OECD Cluster Group Workshop Utrecht, May

Chote R, Emmerson C and Simpson H (2003) *The IFS Green Budget: January 2003* Commentary 92 London: Institute for Fiscal Studies

Corry D (2001) 'Labour's Industrial Policy: a break with the past?' *New Economy 8.3*

Department for Education and Skills (DfES) (2003a) *21st Century Skills: realising our potential* Available at www.dfes.gov.uk/skillsstrategy/

Department for Education and Skills (DfES) (2003b) *The Future of Higher Education* Norwich: The Stationery Office

Department for Education and Skills (DfES) (1999) *Jobs for All: a report of Policy Action Team 1* London: DfES

Department of Trade and Industry (DTI) (2003) *Guide to the Regional Selective Assistance Scheme* Cm 5416 London: DTI

Department of Trade and Industry (DTI) (2002a) *Regional Innovation Performance in the UK* unpublished paper, contact brian.stockdale@dti.gov.uk

Department of Trade and Industry (DTI) (2002b) *Social Enterprise: a strategy for success* London: DTI

Department of Work and Pensions (DWP) (2003) *Households Below Average Income: an analysis of the income distribution from 1994-5 to 2001-02* Leeds: Corporate Document Services

Department of Work and Pension (DWP) (2002) *Client Group Analysis: quarterly bulletin on the population of working age on key benefits* May Newcastle: DWP

Dixon S (2003) 'Migration within Britain for Job Reasons' *Labour Market Trends 111.4*

Employers Skills Survey (2002) *Skills, Local Areas and Unemployment* Warwick: Institute for Employment Research

Engel N (ed) (2002) *Age of Regions: meeting the productivity challenge* London: The Smith Institute

Erdem E and Glyn A (2001) 'Jobs Deficits in UK Regions' in Dickens R, Wadsworth J and Gregg P (eds) *The State of Working Britain: update 2001* London: Centre for Economic Performance, London School of Economics

Eurostat (2002) *Regional Gross Domestic Product in the European Union 1999* Available at www.eu-datashop.de/download/EN/sta_kurz/thema1/_dn_02_01.pdf

Evans M, Noble M, Wright G, Smith G, Lloyd M and Dibben C (2002) *Growing Together or Growing Apart? Geographic patterns of change of Income Support and income-based Jobseeker's Allowance claimants in England between 1995 and 2000* Bristol: The Policy Press/Joseph Rowntree Foundation

Experian Business Strategies (2003) Unpublished data presented at private seminar

Feinstein L (1998) *Pre-School Education Inequality: British children in the 1970 cohort* London: CEPS, London School of Economics

Gibbons M, Limoges C, Nowotny H, Schwartzman S, Scott P and Trow M (1994) *The New Production of Knowledge: the dynamics of science and research in contemporary societies* London: Sage

Gillespie A and Benneworth P (2002) 'Industrial and Regional Policy in a Devolved United Kingdom' in Adams J and Robinson P (eds) *Devolution in Practice: public policy differences within the UK* London: ippr/ESRC

Gordon I (2003) 'One World City, Two World Class Regions: labour market and transport interdependencies between London and its neighbours in South East England' *Paper presented at 'The New Regionalism' conference* Barbican 11 July

Gordon I (2002) 'Industrial and Regional Policy: a London perspective' in Adams J and Robinson P (eds) *Devolution in Practice: public policy differences within the UK* London: ippr/ESRC

Gordon I (1999) 'Targeting a Leaky Bucket: the case against localised employment creation' *New Economy 6.4*

Gordon I, Travers T, and Whitehead C (2002) *London's Place in the UK Economy* London: Corporation of London

Grayling T (forthcoming) 'Whatever Happened to Integrated Transport?' *Political Quarterly*

Grayling T (ed) (2001) *Any More Fares? Delivering better bus services* London: ippr

Green A and Owen D (2002) *Exploring Local Areas, Skills and Unemployment: exploratory data analysis at local area level* Nottingham: Department for Education and Skills

Gregg P (2002) 'Work and Communities' *Paper presented to DTI conference* 15 January

Gregg P, Machin S and Manning A (2001) *Mobility and Joblessness* Copies available from the first author, Department of Economics, University of Bristol

Griliches Z (1996) *Education, Human Capital and Growth: a personal perspective* National Bureau of Economic Research WP 5426

Harding A, Evans R, Parkinson M and Garside P (1996) *Regional Government in Britain: an economic solution?* Bristol: The Policy Press

Heald D and McLeod A (2002) 'Beyond Barnett? Financing devolution' in Adams J and Robinson P (eds) *Devolution in Practice: public policy differences within the UK* London: ippr/ESRC

HM Treasury (HMT) (2003a) *Budget 2003: building a Britain of economic strength and social justice* HC500 London: The Stationery Office

HM Treasury (HMT) (2003b) *Public Expenditure Statistical Analyses 2003* Norwich: The Stationery Office

HM Treasury (HMT) (2002a) *2002 Spending Review: Public Service Agreements 2003-2006* Cm 5571 Norwich: The Stationery Office

HM Treasury (HMT) (2002b) *Opportunity and Security for All: investing in an enterprising, fairer Britain – 2002 Spending Review: new public spending plans 2003-2006* Cm 5570 Norwich: The Stationery Office

HM Treasury (HMT) (2001) *Pre-Budget Report: building a stronger, fairer Britain in an uncertain world* Norwich: The Stationery Office

HM Treasury, the Department of Trade and Industry and the Office of the Deputy Prime Minister (HMT/DTI/ODPM) (2003) *A Modern Regional Policy for the United Kingdom* London: The Stationery Office

HM Treasury and the Department of Trade and Industry (HMT/DTI) (2001) *Productivity in the UK: 3 – the regional dimension* Norwich: The Stationery Office

HM Treasury, the Department of Trade and Industry and the Department for Education and Skills (HMT/DTI/DfES) (2002) *Investing in Innovation: a strategy for science, engineering and technology* Norwich: The Stationery Office

HM Treasury and the Department for Work and Pensions (HMT/DWP) (2000) *The Goal of Full Employment: employment opportunity for all throughout Britain. Trends in regional and local vacancies and unemployment* London: HM Treasury

HM Treasury and the Office of the Deputy Prime Minister (HMT/ODPM) (2003) *Productivity in the UK: 4 – the local dimension* Norwich: The Stationery Office

Hubert F and Pain N (2002) 'Fiscal Incentives, European Integration, and the Location of Foreign Direct Investment' *Working paper* London: National Institute of Economic and Social Research

Institute of Employment Research (2001) *Projections of Occupations and Qualifications 2000/2001, Volume 2* Warwick: Institute of Employment Research

Institute for Public Policy Research (ippr) (2003) *Race Equality and Diversity Taskforce: Private Sector* Available at www.ippr.org/research/files/team19/project93/briefing%20document.doc

Johnson M (2003) *Not Choice But Champion: a new look at secondary admissions in London* Available at www.ippr.org/london

Keating M (2002) 'Devolution and Public Policy in the United Kingdom: divergence or convergence?' in Adams J and Robinson P (eds) *Devolution in Practice: public policy differences within the UK* London: ippr/ESRC

Labour Force Survey (2003) *Labour Force Survey: summary, 1984-2003* Available at www.statistics.gov.uk/STATBASE/tsdataset.asp?vlnk=429

Labour Force Survey (2001) *Labour Force Survey* Available at www.stat.go.jp/english/data/roudou/

Labour Force Survey (1999) *Labour Force Survey* Available at www.stat.go.jp
/english/data/roudou/

Layard R (2003) 'What Would Make a Happier Society?' *Lionel Robbins Memorial Lectures* 5 March London: LSE Available at www.cep.lse.ac.uk/events/lectures/ layard/ RL050303.pdf

Lyons M (2003) *Letter to all Government Departments: Public Sector Relocation Project – further guidance* 10 July London: HM Treasury

MacGillivray A, Potts G and Raymond P (2002) *Secrets of their Success: fast growth business in Britain's inner cities* London: NEF

Machin A (2003) 'The Vacancy Survey: a new series of National Statistics' *Labour Market Trends 111.7*

Mandelson P (2001) 'Keynote Address' *The State of the English Regions Seminar* University of Newcastle-upon-Tyne 21 June

Martin R and Sunley P (2000) 'Deconstructing Clusters: chaotic or policy panacea?' *Journal of Economic Geography 3.1*

McConnell J (2002) 'Funding Devolution: why Barnett remains better than the alternatives' *New Economy 7.2*

McLean I (2003) *Identifying the Flow of Domestic and European Expenditure Into the English Regions* Oxford: Nuffield College

McLean I and McMillan A (2003) 'The Distribution of Public Expenditure Across the UK Regions' *Fiscal Studies 24*

Meager N and Bates P, with Cowling M (2003) 'Business Start-up Support for Young People Delivered by The Prince's Trust: a comparative study of labour market outcomes' *DWP Research report 184* Leeds: Corporate Document Services

Medical Research Council (MRC) (2003) *Medical Research Council Annual Report 2001/02* London: MRC

Michie J and Oughton C (2001) 'Regional Innovation Strategies: integrating regional, industrial and innovation policy' *New Economy 8.3*

Midwinter A (1997) 'The Barnett Formula and Scotland's Public Expenditure Needs' *Treasury Committee on the Barnett Formula Second Report of Session 1997-98 HC 341* London: The Stationery Office

Morgan K (2002) 'The English Question: regional perspectives on a fractured nation' *Regional Studies 36.7*

Morgan K and Rees G (2001) 'Learning by Doing: devolution and the governance of economic development in Wales' in Chaney P, Hall T and Pithouse A (eds) *New Governance – New Democracy* Cardiff: University of Wales Press

National Audit Office (NAO) (2003) 'The Department for Trade and Industry: regional grants in England' *Report by the Comptroller and Auditor General* London: The Stationery Office

National Statistics (ONS) (2003a) *Regional Gross Value Added* Available at www.statistics.gov.uk/pdfdir/gva0803.pdf

National Statistics (ONS) (2003b) *Jobs Densities for Local Areas: a new indicator* Available at www.statistics.gov.uk/articles/nojournal/job_densities_LMTAug03.pdf

National Statistics (ONS) (2003c) 'Table 10.8: aspects of their area that householders would like to see improved' *Social Trends 33* Norwich: The Stationery Office

National Statistics (ONS) (2003d) *Labour Market Trends 111.4*

National Statistics (ONS) (2002) *Regional Trends 37* Available at www.statistics.gov.uk/downloads/theme_compendia/Regional_Trends_37/Regional_Trends_37_contents_revised.pdf

National Statistics and Department for Environment, Food and Rural Affairs (ONS/DEFRA) (2002) *Achieving a better quality of life: review of progress towards sustainable development – Government annual report 2002* London: DEFRA

Nine English Regional Development Agencies (2003) 'Memorandum of the Nine English Regional Development Agencies' in Office of the Deputy Prime Minister Select Committee *Reducing Regional Disparities in Prosperity, Ninth Report of Session 2002-03. Volume 3: oral and written evidence* London: The Stationery Office

North West Development Agency (NWDA) (2003) 'NWDA Invest £35 million into New World-Class University' *Press Release* 1 July Warrington: NWDA

Office of the Deputy Prime Minister (ODPM) (2003a) *Sustainable Communities: building for the future* London: ODPM

Office of the Deputy Prime Minister (ODPM) (2003b) *Creating Sustainable Communities: Thames Gateway and growth areas* London: ODPM

Office of the Deputy Prime Minister Select Committee (2003a) *Reducing Regional Disparities in Prosperity. Volume 1: report* London: The Stationery Office

Office of the Deputy Prime Minister Select Committee (2003b) *Reducing Regional Disparities in Prosperity, Ninth Report of Session 2002-03. Volume 3: oral and written evidence* London: The Stationery Office

Office of the Deputy Prime Minister spokesperson quoted in The Journal (2003) 'Ministry "should go north"' *The Journal* 1 August

Office of the Deputy Prime Minister, HM Treasury, Department for Transport, Core Cities Group, Department for Trade and Industry and England's Regional Development Agencies (2003) *Cities, Regions and Competitiveness: second report from the Working Group of Government Departments, the Core Cities and the Regional Development Agencies* London: ODPM

Office of Science and Technology spokesperson (2003) *Telephone Interview* 14 August

O'Mahoney M and de Boer W (2002) 'Britain's Relative Productivity Performance: updates to 1999. A report for DTI/Treasury/ONS' *Working Paper National Institute for Economic and Social Research* Available at www.niesr.ac.uk/epke/britainRPP.pdf